Jew in the Pew

a memoir

Jenny Berg Chandler

Copyright © 2013 Jenny Berg Chandler

All rights reserved.

ISBN: 0615811019
ISBN 13: 9780615811017

DEDICATION

I dedicate this book to Tim, my dear husband, who is the love of my life. I am incomplete without him. Throughout our marriage he has shown me more unconditional love that I have ever knew existed. Without him there would be no book in your hands.

My love, thank you for all the support and encouragement. This accomplishment is ours together.

CONTENTS

	Acknowledgments	vii
1	The Backstory	1
2	The Timeline	13
3	September	25
4	Time, Forward & Back	39
5	Mascara & Unwanted Gifts	47
6	The Start of the Season	57
7	Research	71
8	Yom Kippur	79
9	Sukkot - Feast Of Tabernacles	93
10	Friday Night Dinners	115
11	Wrestling	129
12	December	141
13	Chanukah	157
14	Forgiveness & MLK	165
15	New Things	179
16	Teaching Moments	189
17	Spring Break & My Brother	199
18	Passover	205
19	Easter	221
20	Conversations	231
21	Full Circle	239
	Epilogue	253
	Extras	257
	About the Author	263

ACKNOWLEDGMENTS

As with any book, no matter how inspired the subject, without the support of certain people it would never happen. The same is true here. I'd like to acknowledge a handful of treasured people who have helped me.

Mom, for your reading, feedback and editing of years of drafts! I can't count how many times and renditions you have seen. You have been unceasingly supportive and have never wavered in your vision of the success of this book. Thank you.

Dad, from the very day you read and edited the manuscript you have been pushing me to get it published. No one I know is as well read as you and your praise and encouragement of my writing, including this book, is a precious gift I hold dear. Thank you.

Emme and Zander, for all the times you gave me space when I was writing. You both were always considerate of that time and never once made me feel guilty (as mother's often do) for working on my own project. I am so proud of you. Thank you.

Sean, for your sincere friendship - all the listening, talking things out, honesty and appreciation. Outside of my family you alone have been unfailingly interested and encouraging. Thank you.

The Jewish Community of Jacksonville, Florida, for being nothing but gracious and accepting of me! What a healing and wonderful thing it has been to be able to be myself, make friends and just be part of the tribe. You are a very special group of people. Thank you.

Jesse Lash for the cover concept, Ryan Schinneller of Image Media Resource for shooting the cover pictures and our dear friends who came to stage it and be supportive. Thank you all.

My grandparents, great-grandparents and lots of aunts and uncles. My mom is the cute little girl in the back.

1
THE BACKSTORY

"IN A BROKEN NEST THERE ARE FEW WHOLE EGGS."
— CHINESE PROVERB

Late August. It feels like it's been summer forever.
I'm ready for a change.

It's an old photo album, spiral bound with a crazy print on the front that made sense in that era of long muumuus, sunken living rooms with shag carpet and avocado appliances in the kitchen. Mostly, it sits completely neglected on my mother's bookshelf in her rented townhouse where she now lives with my grandmother, a ditzy dog named Lizzie and has more than one drawer completely full of vitamins which I'm convinced are never taken.

Every once in a while, like today, I pull the album down and look through it, letting myself be transported back to what I've idealized as a happier time. I'm not sure why I bother because it always makes me feel melancholy. My sister, mother and grandmother are in the kitchen discussing arugula or something. I wander off and find myself diving into the faded pages of times gone by. There are pictures of pool parties with my then much younger grandmother in her rubber bathing cap covered with floppy daisies who's delighted to be with us children. And uncles telling stories while holding cocktails, sitting on folding lawn chairs with strap webbing, their crossed legs showing off plaid shorts with calf-high socks and nubuck shoes. My parents are there too, of course, as their big house was the gathering place of our large extended family.

Even without the help of those yellowed photographs, I recall my father at those gatherings, so handsome and smart, always up for a fun debate, his chesty laugh carrying over the crowd when someone said something especially witty. My father had the

THE BACKSTORY

tight physique of the gymnast he once was, with an uncanny resemblance to a young William Shatner. The weird thing is that he even has that Captain Kirk-like mentality of you've-got-to-be-kidding-if-you-think-I-can't-get-us-out-of-this.

My mother seemed happy and stylish with her long slim legs, short auburn hair that curled around her ears and black cat-eyed glasses, preparing the food for a hoard of relatives she loved. They were a handsome couple and must have looked like they had it all together with us three kids — my older siblings Rick and Ellen and myself — not to mention the eleven acres in the country with the horses and the pool parties and the ski trips in the winter.

Rick is six years older than I am. I wonder what it was like for my parents to have such a precocious first born. Both times I was pregnant, I prayed for an average, laid back child. The smart ones look like you can never really get ahead on the parenting curve. No such luck. Both of my kids are dynamic, highly original, independent thinkers. You'll see that as I go on, especially with our son.

My mother must have known she had no average kid on her hands when three-year-old Rick got his presidents mixed up and called his Lincoln Logs Johnson Blocks. A politically aware toddler is quite an indication, though I'm not sure his intellectual acumen has always served him in life. He gets stuck in his head even more than I do and then his green eyes water with emotions that gurgle up unbidden. He is easily brought down by his hurting heart. A brain with an artist's nature is not always an easy combination.

My sister Ellen, or El, as we all call her, is pretty much just delightful. Between you and me, that just sucks, because I am not. I recently introduced a friend to my sister with the normal pleasantries followed by instructions that said friend was *not* to like Ellen better than me. Everyone laughed (thank God) but I really wasn't kidding. She has a continual happy disposition and thick, wavy golden hair. Again, I do not. My "natural" hair is somewhat akin to a drowned beach rat — sort of stringy and not quite brown and not quite blond. El always sees two sides to every story — the picture of middle children, whereas I am firmly in the call-a-spade-a-spade camp, which somehow always gets me a lecture from someone. I can't tell you how many times I've heard, "Why do ya have to be like that?"

Here is a perfect example... except it didn't happen to me, it happened to my grandmother, who I may add totally understands me. One day, Gra (that's my grandmother) walks into her kitchen to find my grandfather (a.k.a. Pop-Pop) fussing with a "hurt" bird he found outside, which he has gently put in a shoebox. This thing was legs up, x's on the eyes, and not moving. Not exactly a candidate for a rescue. Gra takes one look in the box and says, "George, the bird's

THE BACKSTORY

dead." Pop-Pop turns to her and in all seriousness says, "Why do you always have to be so negative?" Just remembering this as I thumb through the photo album makes me chuckle so I yell into the other room, "Hey, remember the one about Pop-Pop and the dead bird?" There's instant recognition, and I hear laughing as they diverge from their conversational path, now about hormones, to retell the story to each other.

I turn another page in the album and come across a picture of another family event. I can't tell if it's Rosh Hashanah, Passover, or even a birthday but everyone is dressed up and having fun. It's clear that someone clicked the camera in the middle of a story. Pop-Pop with open mouth is gesturing while those on the yellow corduroy sofa and leather corner chair are laughing, straightening the clothes on a little kid or mid-sip of a drink. A cigarette dangles from their other hand. There was a lot of family in those days, mostly from my mother's side. Pop-Pop had something like 50 cousins and Gra had four sisters, all of whom were well endowed, suffocating me in busty face-crushing embraces and noisy kisses on the top of my head, while saying things like, "Oy gut nue,[1] look at that punim[2]!" as their jewelry rattled with their movement. There were second cousins, as well as those who were such dear and long-time friends of

---

1 *Yiddish for "Oh my God!"*
2 *Yiddish for "face"*

my grandparents that they had become like family. And there were the younger first cousins who all ran with my sister and brother while I, the youngest of the entire extended family, could never keep up. It could have been because my little legs only went so fast. But I prefer to remember that it was because I couldn't get through a room full of these wonderful grown-ups without them grabbing me for a hug. Which was true.

Gra and Pop-Pop really seemed to be the hinge pin of all those relationships. My sweet grandmother was loved by one and all. My grandfather constantly needed to be the center of attention. That sounds pretty annoying but, luckily, he had the personality, stories and humor to warrant it. Laughing abounded in the family, not from corny stupid jokes but clever, insightful one-liners bouncing back and forth. This was the big leagues for that kind of humor: Billy Crystal meets Nora Ephron and a maybe a touch of Seinfeld thrown in, but minus the New York accent; throw in Philly instead. You get the picture. It was a big, loud, humorous, opinionated, loving, eating, wonderful, everyone-talking-at-once, extended Jewish family. Quick witted, artsy, involved and smart – these were interesting people who were always interested in things. There were good family times back then. Everyone enjoyed coming together, and I adored being in all that warmth. I remember that just walking into a room filled with these people made me feel safe, loved, funny and valued.

THE BACKSTORY

Farms and sprawling estates abounded in suburban Philadelphia back in the 1970s. Ours was no exception. And there were year round things to do. I flip through more pictures and the memories continue: Us kids picking tomatoes from Dad's garden that was not too far from the horse pasture; everyone in sweaters playing scrabble in front of the big fireplace in the living room where bookshelves lined a whole wall from ceiling to floor; Mom bringing hot chocolate out to us while we were skating on the pond. That sharp twang of the ice settling would always scare me half to death. Another photo brings back times of laying on my back in the soft new Spring grass guessing shapes in the clouds while little white petals from blooming cherry trees floated down toward me.

I can see now what an idyllic life it was. I even had a particularly favorite Maple tree near the barn that was just perfect for climbing, sitting in and thinking. There was something so wonderful about being safely tucked away and hidden in its leaves yet being able to look out at the world from a different angle. The branches on the Maple tree spread out like circular stairs. I had only to jump and catch the bottom branch then swing myself up to climb around the trunk higher and higher, one limb-step after another. When you're a kid, you think times like that would last forever.

"Jenn, will ya let Lizzie out," Mom calls to me. I put the album back. Suddenly, I'm back in the present, aware of the sound of plates being set down on the table, a drawer shutting, and the grinding of the can opener. The focus in the kitchen has turned to tuna fish sandwiches on rye toast.

"It all came to an end when my parents divorced, and my mother moved my brother, sister and me away from our large country house on the hill, with the sunlight streaming in through the long-paned windows, into the city. We left the meadows and big sky to live in an 18-foot-wide row home in a shtetl[3]-like enclave of West Philadelphia. It was a home attached wall to wall to a string of identical houses with four windows in the front and four in the back, though one was covered up in the summer with an air-conditioner, the cord hanging down to a nearby outlet. Instead of hearing the wind through the grass or rustle the tops of trees, city buses roared by our tiny brick house belching fumes at every stop. And although we did back up to a municipal golf course, there was never again another special tree in which to sit and process how I saw the world. Along with the loss of parental accord and the country home was the loss of the big extended Jewish family. It completely disintegrated. Well, I suppose that isn't quite true. My grandmother's sisters and their respective families went on with each other. But not with us. We must have been like Typhoid Mary since they just cut us off. Seriously, why do that to people you love? I get

---

3 *Yiddish: Jewish village in Eastern Europe*

THE BACKSTORY

the fact that I was a kid then and not privy to how awkward things may have been and, I know, divorce is hard on everyone. But still. Maybe the divorce plus the whole Jesus thing was just too much. I guess I should be more gracious and understanding now that I think back on it all.

My parents' religious differences really ended their marriage. Isn't that sad? Sure, there were other things but that was really the last straw, apparently. Here's the short version. Mom accepted that Jesus is the Messiah. Although very involved in synagogue, she had been searching for a greater sense of God and purpose for many years. Trying to be a good person, or raising money for Israel, didn't fill the void for her. I can't remember the name of the lady she met who told her about Jesus.... was her name Matilde? No. Maxine maybe? Oh, I don't know. I saw her once or twice when she came to the house. A great big fat lady with white hair and pale skin who reminded me of uncooked bread like when Mom made challah and let dough rise between kneading. She and mom would sit and have these long conversations. It's not exactly an easy thing for a Jew to wrap her head around the idea that the Christian God on the cross in whose name we have been persecuted was really the one we've been looking and waiting for all these millennia.

But she was convinced and prayed The Prayer and that was it. She became a believer and never looked back, with nothing less than fervor. Anyone who meets her hears that right away. Like last week, when we were in an art gallery in St Augustine. El and I were dreamily taken in by a painting of rain washed city streets as lovers strolled by storefronts, arms around each other under an umbrella. It was such a wonderful scene, I turned to call Mom's attention to it but saw she was deep in conversation with the art director about his religious beliefs, a man she had just met. I felt my body go from expectant sharing to shoulder dropping as I turned back to El and the painting. Sometimes, I look at my mother and wonder if she had been as devoted about anything else in her life before this transformation. I know there is a quilt in her closet that she has been trying to finish since 1973, so maybe not.

Dad was not interested in such God nonsense. He thinks it is hubris to believe in a personal savior. Not that he was an observant Jew; he wasn't and still isn't. He is culturally Jewish, not spiritually. Here are some examples: He went to law school, made lots of money in real estate, bagels and lox on the weekends is a must, has bookshelves full of topics like Hitler, Germany and the Jews, is still disappointed that I didn't become a doctor and even in the way he pronounces Flahidah (Florida).

Thankfully, the exceptions to our familial alienation were my afore mentioned mother's parents, Gra and Pop-Pop, and her brother, Michael. Just a few years prior to this, he had finally returned home from being the quintessential hippie, following the Guru Maharaja, bathing in the Ganges river, spending a lot of time focusing on his third eye and saying things like, "That's heavy, man." They were the only relatives we now saw at holidays. It all felt so abrupt and lonely and painful and confusing. I was seven year old.

THE TIMELINE

fundamentals like crossing a city street without getting hit, I loved living in that neighborhood, and knowing so many people. It was especially nice to sometimes walk to services on Friday nights with other Jews walking to their shuls[6] too.

Within a year of our move, my grandparents, Gra and Pop-pop, also embraced Messianic Judaism and, in support of my mother and to be close to us kids, sold their house and bought the row home that shared a wall with ours, right next door. It was great! We enjoyed living life together. To me it meant school treats of Peanut Butter Tastycakes, Shabbat meals with a challah from Greenberg's Bakery, helping Gra bring the groceries in from the car, hearing Pop-Pop play his cello through the walls, climbing onto Gra's big bed with the yellow bedspread to watch M*A*S*H* with them and laugh with Pop-Pop as he cried at sentimental commercials. They were a major influence in my life, which explains why I sometimes sound like a 65 year old, and why I know so much Yiddish.

So, although we lost our extended big family, we gained a much closer relationship with my grandparents and a Jewish community that also felt familial. In many ways it was as before where I ran

---

6 *Shul is Yiddish for synagogue. At that time, this area of West Philly was mostly Jewish complete with Kosher butcher, Jewish deli, baker, a Jewish Community Center, and both Orthodox and Conservative synagogues.*

around in the midst of talking adults who would hug me or tousle my hair as I went by, sharing holidays and life events together. I've painted an idyllic picture for you but even so, life had its problems — like the Catholic neighbor who didn't like us, my father's anger that Mom moved us to a row home in the city, a few control freaks in the congregation and Pop-Pop's petulance when he felt he wasn't being paid enough attention.

Fast-forward twenty-five years. I've been married to my high-school sweetheart for a long time now. When I started going to a new school in ninth grade, he was the guy with the locker right next to mine. Oh, I couldn't even breathe around him because he was so cute. And, even worse, I kept dropping my books. I remember being on the phone with my brother, who was at college in Boston at the time, telling him about Tim: "He's really, like, cute and has dark hair and brown eyes. And is, like, um, kinda built like Dad, ya know? All, like, short and muscular. And he runs track and ... " Rick must have enjoyed hearing his 14 year old sister gush on and on about a guy. I had never before shared boy stuff with him.

As High School unfolded, Tim and I became best friends, though frustratingly platonic. I dated someone horrible and he dated someone very nice (i.e. boring) and we would talk to each other about that. He would show me the cards or little something he bought Melanie and I would tell him what a jerk Roy was

THE TIMELINE

being. We just enjoyed spending time together and learning about each other's very different worlds. I was fascinated to hear about how his mom did breakfast like June Cleaver — scrambled eggs on Mondays, pancakes on Tuesdays, oatmeal on Wednesdays, etc. He thought my passionate and opinionated family was interesting. I lived in a row home with my mother in the city yet had a father who lived on an estate in the country who would do things like take me to Europe on Thanksgiving weekends, while Tim lived in a ranch house in suburbia with Ozzie and Harriet, mowed the lawn on weekends, went to church and finished his vegetables. He wasn't all goody two shoes. After all, he did let me cheat off him in Biology and helped me pass Spanish. To this day, my entire Spanish vocabulary consists of hola, noches and tacos. Not to mention the time we skipped school to go into town for a Ferris Bueller kind of day or when we pinched a half empty bottle of rum from my dad's liquor cabinet — all of which were my ideas, I must admit.

For the rest of high school we got closer and closer, periodically talking about how great it was to be just friends. Yeah, right. By senior year we had an elephant in the room with us — what do you do when you are in love with your platonic best friend? It was like one of those teenage romantic comedies where she would be in her bedroom with her girlfriend trying to come up with crazy ways to make this work out but she knows it's just impossible and flops on her bed in despair. Meanwhile, back at his house he is convincing his parents that the friend he wants to bring on their family trip to Disney during Spring Break is her: "Dad, really, I don't like her like that. Honest." Both sets of parents finally agree and off we go.

After a series of ridiculous car problems on the 900 mile car ride that only happened when it was Tim's turn to drive — we run out of gas, a tire blows, the keys get locked in the trunk, we have to sleep in the car at a gas station in the middle of nowhere, the windows won't roll down (and I'm claustrophobic), Tim and I finally have a day by ourselves walking around Epcot.

And then it happened. Right there in Paris, on a black wrought iron bench, with background music and swans gliding on the nearby lakes. Ok, there was also that fat, loud kid shoving éclairs in his mouth but we ignored him. For two days we had been talking about prom coming up and who Tim wanted to ask but wasn't sure if he should. We toyed with the topic for hours while waiting in lines here and there. I couldn't stand it anymore. Taking a deep breath, I finally said, "Tim, is it me?" Fat kid screams for his mommy when he drops his food on the ground. Then it's all quiet again, there's only that piped in quintessential French music. "Of course it's you," he said softly.

And so I hit him. Why didn't he just tell me that in the first place! He laughed, rubbed his arm and kissed me for the first time. It felt like a puzzle piece that I didn't even know was missing suddenly went into place. We got up, held hands and floated around the rest of the park, not seeing a thing. To this day, I still wonder what took him so long to tell me. We got married three years and three months later on a sunny June day, just after we turned 21.

My family was fine with the fact that Tim isn't Jewish, because he is such a mensch[7]. However, Pop-Pop did think it was important to ask me if he was circumcised in front of everyone at Shabbat dinner one night. Gra quickly jumped in, "Oy, George, what kind of questions is that. (Pause) So, is he?" And the whole table stops eating to wait for my answer. Just the conversation every 18-year-old girl wants to have with her grandfather. "Yes, Pop-Pop. Can we drop it now?"[8]

Tim and I have two children. Our first born, (Emily?) Emme, or "Em," as we call her, at 12 years of age, is a dark haired beauty. She is opinionated, spirited, strong, independent and emotional with a wry sense of humor. I must tell you that she gets constantly compared to her mother with those same attributes. Her love of sports sets her apart from the rest of our non-sporty household. Lately she spends a

---

[7] *Yiddish = Honorable, upstanding, wonderful person, literally, a man (of quality).*

[8] *I wanted to just let the question hang but since both of our mothers will read this... I knew because I had asked him long before we were ever a couple. He was my best friend, after all.*

lot of time banging a volleyball against the side of the house. Frankly, balls kind of scare me. They have this tendency to hit me in the head. Besides, sports seem to always include sweating, something I try to avoid.

Zander, which is short for Alexander, is such a leader-type. He is always busy building, doing, talking, climbing, dismantling, figuring things out, and telling people where to go or how to get things done. I first noticed this when he was three years old. It occurred to me that every time I looked out the window to our backyard gaggle of little neighbors playing, he was always the ringleader. And all of those kids were older than he, some as old as eight. It was weird.

When Zander was five years old, we remodeled our kitchen. At some point during the day, I realized I didn't hear him — an unusual occurrence because he always makes a lot of noise, so the silence meant I better go see what he was up to. He wasn't in his room constructing elaborate train tracks, and he wasn't in the basement rearranging furniture to build a fort. I found him in his tree house where he was busily dry walling the inside, complete with hammer in hand and nails held in the corner of his mouth, just like he saw the big guys do. I must say, it was a pretty good job, too, considering the hammer was the size of his thigh. This apple doesn't fall far from the tree. Tim told me that when he was a kid, his dad found him running electricity to his tree house.

I cannot neglect to mention one more hugely important 'person' in our household. Twenty-five pounds of love and acceptance covered in fur — our Beagle. Otis, like Tim, is patient, kind and loved by all. It is an added bonus that he understands English fluently. The dog, I mean.

Now, here's a crazy thing: We now live just outside of Historic St Augustine in Florida. Were on a small and somewhat rural peninsula that juts out into the Atlantic where the sun both rises and sets over water. I say that because, really, who lives that way? Sure, all of my neighbors do but still it seems kind of ridiculously lucky. Sometimes I stand in our driveway where I can hear the ocean just two blocks away and think about how I could still be up in Pennsylvania with the cold and the frequently grey skies and the sinus pressure. Often Otis and I take a stroll toward the Intracoastal Waterway that is banked by sweeping, marsh views or we walk along the beach. See? Crazy.

Walking is a huge pleasure for me. I need that space to think and relax and process because, to use Tim's analogy, I always have too many programs running at one time in my head. He tells me that I need to shut them down; I tell him that I really can only minimize them but they will still be humming in the background. Going for a walk lets me re-prioritize as my eyes and mind wander over the wide expanse of grasses, water and sky. Occasionally the view is peppered by a hawk gliding on unseen air currents

JEW IN THE PEW

or white herons doing their high stepping tip-toe through the wetlands, while Fiddler Crabs sideways-scurry always just out of Otis's reach.

Over the bridge is St Augustine[9], a quaint 500-year-old town. A rarity of age in our country. I read somewhere that it was voted the most European-like city in the U.S. It has little cobblestone streets, old buildings leaning together, with shops, restaurants and ornate stone churches. It is a beautiful place — quaint, full of history, and small-town, American charm. You have it made here if you are Catholic — schools for your kids, parishes for your religious needs, and lots of community involvement. But what if you are Jewish? Uh, well then, not so much is going on here though I hear there is a tiny, old synagogue tucked away on a downtown side street somewhere.

My sister and her four children, my mother and Gra (Pop-Pop died seven years ago) migrated south too, although they all live about an hour away in Jacksonville. But even though I have some family here and live at the beach (a dream come true), there is still a melancholy that hangs about my thoughts. The cause: We go to church, not synagogue and, I'm just not okay with the way our religious life is

---

9 *Founded in 1565 by the Spanish Admiral Pedro Menendez on the Feast Day of St Augustine, which means it predates the Virginian Jamestown colony by forty-two years and Plymouth Rock by fifty-five. It is the oldest continuously occupied European settlement in America.*

playing out. That is a pretty important piece for me. We're basically living a lifestyle that is immersed in Christianity. To put it mildly, it's kind of freaking me out. One, I really miss Jewish things – like other Jews, holidays, culture, food, etc., and two, I'm incredibly concerned about our children's lack of Jewish identity. I keep wondering if my kids even understand what it means to be Jewish, since I am raising them in church. What part of Judaism do I want to instill in our lives? And how should I go about doing that? At every Christian holiday I feel like a foreigner who doesn't belong there. At every Jewish holiday I feel let down, and sad that I don't celebrate within a community of our own (besides our immediate family), while sharing life-cycle events and annual feasts. This plays out over and over again throughout the year.

Even though I have long been a committed believer in Yeshua (Jesus), I'd like to publicly admit that for some time now I have wanted way more than what mainstream Christianity doles out. I want my heritage back.

3
SEPTEMBER

"FEW THINGS DEFINE US MORE THAN HOW WE STRUGGLE."
– BETH MOORE

Early September. It's damp and blustery outside;
as if a storm is coming.

This morning I went to the bookstore to pick out a new journal. It took nearly an hour to find the perfect fit. Finally, with joy like that widow in the Bible who found her lost coin, there it was on the shelf, the right size — not too big, with the right paper — lined and smooth, covered in red embossed leather! I tried not to skip my way to the register while singing. In my head, though, it was scene from a musical with a backup chorus and possibly guys in tights leaping in unison.

JEW IN THE PEW

The other night, I used the last page in my journal. It's where I write the stuff that just feels too raw to say out loud. Not exactly secret things, more like my own *drek*[10] that I know no one else wants to hear about. Again. My last entry was written with a heavy hand, the words were practically carved into the paper about this ongoing and increasingly deep, soul-identity, ache.

There is something magical about writing thoughts down. What has felt too *verboten* to say out loud is finally articulated on the page. Lately, I really need to verbalize what has been building in my heart to see if I can untangle these muddled strands. Maybe it sounds crazy that a believer should feel at a loss over identity. You know, a big tag line for evangelistic thinking seems to be, "Accept Jesus and you'll never feel lost/alone/empty again." It's very true. To an extent. I never feel devoid of the presence of God; He is always with me. But I do feel like a doll made out of unmatched parts wandering around, checking out the other toys to see how they are put together, and if they match up.

I can't tell you how many Christians have told me they think it's such a cool thing to possess both halves — the Jewish and the Christian. I appreciate their interest and support but it makes me feel kind of different too. They look at me with such enthusiasm, as if I am about to unfold an ancient secret of the

---

10 *Yiddish: ...um... let's say it means excrement*

intersection between two powerful religions. They're right, there is an element of truth there. I do have the best of both worlds. After all, Jesus was a Jew and when you see the interweaving between the Jewish Bible (the Old Testament) and the Christian New Testaments it's quite a love story. So then why does it make me feel lonely? I'm not sure I can even articulate it. It's an emotion that just drifts in at those times, like dark clouds moving in from the horizon. Which reminds me, I better take Otis for a walk soon before it rains.

I'll tell you what I find seriously odd though — and, sure, maybe this is just switching tracks because I can't yet answer my own question — it's that your average Christian seems to have only a vague idea about the Jewish foundations of their own beliefs. There is also lacking any real concept of the church's anti-Semitic history. Most Jews know more about this grievous part of Church history than many Christians do — probably because it is taught to them in a sort of "...And let's not forget what the Christians did to us... we gotta watch out for them so they don't do it again" way.

Wait a sec; maybe these two thoughts do go together. I think I feel lonely because I see how much teaching has to come first. Even though so many Christian leaders profess support and love for the Jewish people, without taking the time to teach their congregants, I feel slightly patronized. "Yes, we care about the Jews but we have more important things to do than teach our own history regarding them." To really explain why I feel weird, or sad, being a Jew in a church would take first giving a bit of a history lesson to friendly Mr. Christian and I confess that sometimes I'm just not up to the challenge. I think I'll just come across sounding bitter, which possibly I am.

Time for a little gardening, planting pansies in little clusters here and there so they look at if they naturally grew there.

On my way to the backyard I knocked over my St. Francis statue with a big bag of mulch. That would be pretty Freudian if I was a struggling Catholic. But I'm not. I'm a Jew with a decorative but chipped Patron Saint who blindly oversees my seaside garden of ferns, lavender and rosemary. To be honest, the poor thing wasn't in the best shape to begin with. I bought him on clearance at a garden center where he was marked down 70%. Based on how my roses look I'm guessing the big chunk missing near his feet has negated his ability to ward off aphids.

Shortly after we moved here, Mary, a neighbor who is Catholic, asked my husband Tim what we were. She said, "I'm confused. Here is a garden statue of St. Francis, but you're not Catholic. Jenny mentioned she was Jewish, but you go to a non-denominational church." Why didn't I see that question coming when I plunked Frankie down there by the sprawling Mexican petunia in the front yard? I've since moved the statue to the back yard where I don't need to defend his marred existence. I've also renamed him Saint Frank *Greenberg*.

Oh. If only dealing with this whole religious quandary of mine was as easy as moving a decorative piece of plaster. Wouldn't that be great? I can't tell you how many times I tried to walk away from dealing with the question of where I belong. I feel a little like that children's story of the little bird that walks around asking, "Are you my mother?" It's particularly tragic when he asks the cold and silent backhoe. That part gets me every time — a metaphor for modern life and the search for identity. So maybe not a direct parallel because one, I'm not a bird and, two, I know my mother. But, I am a Jewish believer navigating through life in a Gentile Christian world feeling nestless. I'm not really sure what the backhoe symbolizes.

There are different schools of garden design — make it look as if you have conquered nature or make it look like nature idealized. I choose the latter. As I try to choose which color pansy will look as if it really fits in which spot, my friend Daniel pops into my head. Not because he is a gardener too. He's not. He was a missionary for many years in Costa Rica who happens to think he has the answer to my disquiet. He says that once you have been immersed in multiple cultures, you can only hope for a mixture but can't ever be of just one again. Yea, that's great, Daniel, and probably true, but that just doesn't cut it. For one thing, it's over simplifying the situation. I'm not just talking about culture. I'm talking about *God* and heritage and how to raise my children! With that thought, I jab the ground with my trowel, hit a buried rock that flicked some dirt in my eye. Oh damn.

Trying to find something on TV while I'm ironing. Seems that there are only shows about people who behave badly or who have overcome some terrible tragedy.

It is so stupid that I iron Tim's shirts. I should just send them out but then I feel guilty because there's no reason that I can't just do it myself. There is no way my mother-in-law ever spent money on something she could just do herself. Hence, in some sort of weird unspoken competition between the generations, I begrudgingly iron.

Tim was raised Baptist. They were at church three nights a week, no drinking, dancing or cursing, staunch Republicans, weekend chores; and dessert only if you finished your dinner. These were a strong work ethic kind of people. I was raised less than an hour away, but a world apart. My people — specifically my father and maternal grandfather —

overcame Dickens-like bad childhoods to become ballsy, outside the box, highly creative, self-made, real estate-niks. They also had very crisp dress shirts that came straight from the cleaners.

Given the differences in our families of origin, it's odd how perfect Tim and I are for each other. You might have picked up on the fact that I am a little high strung. Well, Tim has a profound calming effect on me. Think the horse whisperer but he's like the Jenny whisperer. I'd still be wild-eyed animal in a corner of the pasture who rears up and paws the sky when spooked if it wasn't for him. "Shhh... it's okay, Jenny... don't worry... shhhh..." You may be wondering why I even need such a reassuring presence.

Get a cup of coffee. It's a bit of a long story.

Like I said, I was raised Messianic — except for those early years in Reform Judaism — and lived in a very tight-knit Jewish neighborhood, complete with a delicatessen supplying our lox, knishes and corned beef needs and the butcher shop that had the Hebrew word "kosher" in neon in the window. It was a small and insular community. Even our black lab, Boaz, was well known at the back door of Greenberg's Bakery where he frequently got a little *schnecken*[11]. One day, I was walking by and, there he was, getting his treat. Who knew? I had always wondered where he'd been when he'd come home with a jaunty, 'just-had-a-nice-snack' air about him.

---

11 *A German-Jewish pastry*

JEW IN THE PEW

I am sure that I would have stayed in Messianic Judaism forever, but something sort of cataclysmic happened. For years — really, a huge chunk of my childhood — we went to synagogue there. Up until high school, I attended their Jewish day school. My friends were all from the congregation. During the summer, we always attended the international Messianic conference and my family was well known in these circles. I faintly remember being interviewed for some TV show, because we represented three generations of Jewish Believers, something unheard of in the late 70's.

Pop-Pop had done the amazing thing of buying the building for our congregation. Every time the members tried to buy it, a room full of angry Conservative Jews attended the zoning hearing, and thwarted their progress because they didn't want Jews who believed in Jesus in their neighborhood. My grandfather, being the real estate broker he was and *mensch*[12], just came in and bought the building. He then turned it over to the congregation. They paid him back within six months. (Would a little plaque somewhere have killed them? Just saying.)

Mom was the assistant editor of a magazine called *The American Messianic Jew.* At the national conference, she also ran the art show that displayed Messianic art in pen and ink, or watercolor; etchings

---

12 *Yiddish = Honorable, upstanding, wonderful person.*

and oil paintings; and metal or paper sculptures. I was very proud of her and loved to look at the artwork.

Even though there have been always been Jews who believed in Jesus[13], after the first century, there weren't enough of us to make it a movement. And history tells the story of how the Jews (and things Jewish) were ousted from the church. For a very long time Jewish believers had to keep their faith a secret or divorce their heritage and go into churches. But by the 1980's things began to change. We were really up and running, so to speak, though it was still difficult. People didn't know what Messianic Judaism was, and too much pressure was put on us kids to show the Jews we were still Jewish even though we believed in Jesus, and the Christians that we really were believers. I guess people couldn't wrap their head around the fact that you can be both. Though let's remember Jesus was.

With the exception of one friend with whom I've recently reconnected, the spiritual lives of many of my peers from those early years were ground up by the shifting gears — they still bear the scars, and deeply resent that *that* was how they were raised. My brother included. In fact, don't even get him started on the subject. If you do, at

---

13 *The disciples, for example, were Jews who believed in Jesus and for the first century or so the "church" was mostly Jewish.*

least, wear a spit shield to protect you from the spewing vitriol. Which reminds me, I must buy more spray starch.

One Friday I came home from school and found my mother crumpled in a chair, her face mottled from the combination of tears and mascara with a wad of tissues in her hand. She told me that we were leaving the congregation, and on Monday I would be going to a new school. Something about her having a different opinion of how things should be, and how I was being overburdened with too many "shoulds" verses a relationship with God. Was it her decision? Were we asked to leave? What the hell happened? I never felt like I really understood what went down exactly. Mom seemed alone and pretty shattered. Again.

So that was it. It happened in a day. I was 14 years old.

The news went around the Messianic world. We were out.

One sanctimonious power usurper told my friends that they must not even speak to me. Though my friend Rachel braved it and came to say goodbye. It was as if I had been standing there surrounded by packing boxes while the moving van was idling outside. I wasn't. In fact, I lived in that same house in that same neighborhood, just blocks away from everyone else until I graduated high school. There were bad times when someone we knew would see Mom and me on the street and quickly turn away. Once again, where before our home was filled with the bustle and noise of friends, family and events, life had fallen suddenly silent and barren-like. It was as if a bulldozer razed the land — all the trees and growth was gone, nothing looked the same.

I had no words to ask questions. I simply didn't have the language with which to express what I felt. Words like anger, bitterness, sadness, depression, fear, self-rejection, and confusion are all fine and descriptive but now, looking back, I realize that all I felt was shock. As if you just lopped off my arms and I just stood there staring at the spot where I was once someone intact and realizing that all of a sudden I was without, radically different, altered... and bleeding.

It's surprising that I never lost my faith through all that. I just figured people are jerks, hurtful and untrustworthy. I didn't have a problem with God. Him I liked. And I knew that God was the only one who would, or could, be with me deep down where it really hurt. It seemed to me that God understood pain, though I'm not sure why I felt that.

By my late teens, I was so frustrated with being different. I still felt such suspicion from the "regular" Jews, and misunderstanding from the Christians, that I decided Messianic Judaism was a stupid, half-breed, religious answer that wasn't worth the trouble and maybe I should just try to be a bland regular 'ole Christian. It's interesting that it didn't occur to me to become a regular 'ole Jew. That is probably because almost everyone I knew and to whom I was close in Messianic Judaism was Jewish and everything we did was Jewish with the exception of worshipping Jesus who we called by his Hebrew name of Yeshua. I suppose the Christian thing gave me more emotional distance from Big Wound #2. Or would that haven been Big Wound #3?

After Tim and I married, we attended an Episcopal church where, for several years, I tried to embrace the Anglican-Christian culture. I liked the structure of its liturgy, the dignity of the architecture, and the peace in the eighty-year-old chapel, though I still found going to church a slightly foreign and difficult thing. But for the most part, nothing new happened there and there were no surprises[14]. And it was over in an hour and a half, counting the talking to people afterwards. Our Episcopalian friends had a lack of prudeness that I appreciated. Sure, they were impossibly *goyishe*,[15] but in an enviable golf, cocktails and prep school kind of way. There were many times during our Episcopal stint that I even wished I wasn't Jewish, so I could blithely sail along their liturgical calendar as they seemed to do. Since our immediate family never gave up Passover and the like, my year was still punctuated by holidays that said, "They tried to kill us, God showed up, let's eat[16]."

---

14 *This was before the division over whether a gay man could be an ordained priest.*

15 *Yiddish: Gentile*

16 *That would be Passover, Chanukah and Purim. Even though we went to church there, we always celebrated the*

SEPTEMBER

Deep down I knew the Episcopal thing wasn't a perfect fit, that I was square peg in a round hole. Or, more like a short, busty peg in a pert-nose, (naturally) blond hair, and long bone-structure type hole.

Even before we moved to Florida, I was feeling that it was getting to be time to re-address our spiritual life as my long dormant Jewish gland was beginning to work again after so many years. It all would have been easier if, when we moved south, we had relocated to a Northern-Jewish transplant city like Boca or Fort Lauderdale. Nope. We, in an unexplainable transition, moved to good old boy, Bible-belt country – pulled pork and crucifixes, y'all. Now, we attend a church a half-hour away toward Jacksonville where I am the only Jew in the place. This is sooo getting old.

Now, it's September and the autumn Jewish holidays[17] are coming up in a couple of weeks, the kids are getting older and their ignorance of their heritage is starting to upset me. It's one thing if I'm not so good at keeping up on the ironing, it's quite another if I raise kids who don't really know what it means to be a Jew.

Jewish holidays with my family.
17 *Rosh Hashanah, Yom Kippur, Sukkot.*

4
TIME, FORWARD & BACK

"NOT ALL WHO WANDER ARE LOST."
— *J.R.R. TOLKIEN*

The kids went back to school this morning and the house is quiet once again which means I can think and write. Finally.

I yell at Emme to stop talking to her brother like that, they look at the clock, grab their things and run. The door slams shut and silence suddenly descends on the kitchen. I look around at the dishes with half eaten eggs and a counter full of crumbs from making sandwiches for lunch. The pantry door is left open. A few pens are strewn around trying to find one that actually works to sign a permission slip. Cleaning up the mess I think about the kids.

JEW IN THE PEW

Em is just on the cusp of becoming a teenager. Her room is a messy jumble of her exploding drawers and closet. She thinks we are beginning to make unreasonable decisions, and apparently something is wrong with her eyes because she keeps rolling them while sighing.

Zan, our shortening of his already shorted name, is ten now. The whole world is one big place to explore for him. We just try to keep up. The other day, I was talking on the phone to a friend while pulling the mail out of our box, when I glanced up and heard myself say, "Yeah, I gotta go. Zander's coming down the street with a shark. I'll call ya later." It was a small one but still...

I pour a cup of coffee and head to the back door, "Come on Otis, let's go outside." He gets up from the sofa, where he has been patiently waiting for the chaos and clean up to end and follows after me. We pad along the stone path to sit on the little bridge by the koi pond, feeding Jack and Jill their morning fishy flakes. Otis has his nose up, sniffing the salty air coming in off the ocean. It's bright and sunny and somehow reminds me of a day long ago, when I was five.

Mom was washing the breakfast dishes after Rick and Ellen had left for school, looking out the window over the sink to the horse pasture. I, however, was up to something — playing with her make up when I was told not to[18]. The bright coral lipstick that said Bonnie Bell on the side dragged on like a soft waxy crayon. But it didn't make me happy like I thought. Feeling sad and heavyhearted, I rubbed a piece of toilet paper across my lips and cheeks and went to tell my mother what I did. At the edge of the kitchen, I brushed the hair out of my eyes, straightened my shoulders and marched myself in to talk to her. I needed Mom to say that it was okay and that she forgave me. She just looked down at me, dried off her hands and asked if I would like to have a picnic outside.

Confused but excited, I ran upstairs to get my favorite nubby yellow sweater. It was the one that Gra knitted just for me, and not a hand-me-down. That Pennsylvania autumn day was bright and sunny like it is today, with similar fluffy clouds. We sat on a blanket spread out under a Maple tree that still had leaves precariously dangling from its branches. Colors of russet and gold pirouetted overhead, while we ate Ritz crackers *shmeared* with peanut butter.

Mom started to explain. Even though she forgave me for disobeying her about the makeup, there was someone else I needed to ask to forgive me. I felt my furrowed brow bump up against my bangs. *Who could she mean? Did she share makeup with someone else?* She

---

18 *Seriously? Tell a little girl that make up is off limits?! What kind of rule is that? It's ok, Mom, I'm over it. We all make mistakes in our parenting.*

kept talking. *God had a son? Really? I didn't know that! There weren't any pictures of Him in my Children's Jewish Bible.* I had gone through it so often that pages were falling out of the binding. Sitting cross-legged on my white four-poster bed, I'd stare at the faces of people trying to understand what they were feeling. I remember thinking that Adam and Eve looked really upset.

But with all the stories and pictures of the Garden of Eden, Abraham and Moses and all that, I never saw one about God's son or that He cared about me specifically. Yet, here Mom was telling me that God wanted to be close to me again after I had done something wrong, and that His son helps with that. It made sense to me and I was happy to pray with her. I liked prayers and God stuff. The very instant after we prayed I felt happy and lovey inside. I tried really hard not to smile because we had been talking about serious things but I couldn't hold it in. Up crept a huge smile across my face, and we started to laugh together.

Chuckling out loud at the memory, Otis looks at me for explanation. That experience has colored my entire life, not that he'd understand. "Time to get to work. That article isn't going to write itself." Otis gets up and heads inside ahead of me.

TIME, FORWARD & BACK

My turn to drive carpool home today. Nothing quite like an hour in a minivan full of hungry and rowdy pubescent kids after a warm and long day at school.

I'm sorry. The smell was just too much. I actually made one of the kids in our carpool, hold his gym shoes out the window during the ride home. Good thing he didn't drop them. His mother, a level headed woman who has a much higher tolerance for sporty boy smells, would not have been happy.

Emme and Zan are currently attending a private Christian college-prep school. It's got that whole preppy thing going on: girls in plaid skirts and knee-hi's and boys with cropped hair, khaki pants in blue crested blazers. Everyone is really well scrubbed. It *seems* like a great school.

I'm now sitting out back, leaving the kids inside to devour after-school snacks and watch loud mindless TV. The car ride home was enough quality time. I just need a few minutes here. The clouds are starting to look ominous. It was such a lovely day a few minutes ago. What happened? Otis is standing at the back door waiting for me to let him in. "Hold on a sec, I'm writing," I tell him. He sighs and sits down.

I have some hesitations about sending them to that school. And not just because too many of those kids have designer backpacks. Who knew Louis Vuitton had a kid's line? When I share my concerns with my closest Christian friends, though, they are completely

JEW IN THE PEW

perplexed. To them, a Christian kid going to a Christian school is a no-brainer, like Democrats driving Volvos or separating your whites when doing laundry. They don't seem to comprehend how important it is that our heritage is not being supported, or valued in Christian culture when so much of it has Jewish roots. They mean well, of course, but it becomes very myopic to them — you believe in Jesus so nothing else should matter.

A cloud crosses in front of the sun and a shadow falls where I'm now sitting. Suddenly the temperature changes. I'm going to have to go back in soon to start dinner and argue about homework. Otis just looked up at me. How did he know what I was thinking? "No, not yet." He lies back down.

We decided to send them to this great school but real questions nag at me: Are my children the only Jewish kids there? Am I doing the right thing by increasing their Gentile-Christian influences, versus learning what it means to be Jewish? The school calendar has classes scheduled during Jewish holidays; how are we going to handle that? Will my kids grow up and marry Gentile believers instead of Jewish believers, causing even more dilution of Jews in the world? 5,000 years of history and I dropped the ball! *Oy, vey iz mir*[19].

It feels like there is a riptide pulling the sand out from under my feet. I've been sitting in church

---

19 *Yiddish expression of woe is me.*

and playing along for years, but I just can't continue. Church involvement through Sunday school and Youth Group supports our teaching the kids about Jesus but not really in His context; a fact I find baffling. It's as if Jesus was *not* a Jewish man who came from a Jewish family, and talked, ate and worshipped as a Jew and spouted Jewish scripture. There is nary a mention of the holidays[20] when they come around, or teaching of all the Jewish idioms and references Jesus made nor any talk of Israel's importance to God. Wouldn't it make sense for a Christian school or church to teach that which He held dear? How do you love someone and yet disregard who they are and where they came from? Not to mention what's vitally important to them.

I am profoundly bothered by this current lack of Jewish expression in my family's lives. The high cost of tuition for the fancy private school is one thing. But I'm not sure this is the price we should pay for believing in Yeshua[21].

I just heard thunder. "Otis! Let's go!"

---

20 *Rosh Hashanah, Yom Kippur, Sukkot, Chanukah, Purim (these two are not mentioned in Torah but Jesus still celebrated them), Passover, Shavuot...*

21 *Yeshua is His Hebrew name. No one actually called Him Jesus, ya know.*

Our wedding

5

MASCARA & UNWANTED GIFTS

"WHAT SOAP IS FOR THE BODY, TEARS ARE FOR THE SOUL."
— JEWISH PROVERB

Unpacking. Suitcases laying open with party clothes and casual things from our trip strewn all over the closet floor. Can't find my favorite shoes. Where are they?!

Honestly, this is ridiculous. I am just not somebody who loses things. I make lists, know where I put things, organize my closet by color, etc... For example, in my entire life I have only lost one earring and that was because I wasn't watching where I was going, being deep in thought at the time, and slammed into a low tree branch. That earring flew off and into a pile of leaves somewhere. And, now, my comfy everyday shoes are nowhere to be found but I know I packed them!

This past weekend, Tim and I flew up to Philly for the wedding of my oldest friend. Stacy and I have known each other since we were six years old and she still never lets me forget how I landed on her head 27 years ago when I convinced her to help me over some fence. Our families attended the same Messianic synagogue, and we have stayed friends ever since. Through the Barbie years when I had the Barbie corvette but she had that cool folding wardrobe; and then the tween years when we decided to sell barrettes we made with trailing ribbons and beads; the teen years when we'd talk about boys and sex and get hysterical laughing; the college years of thinking we had our act together when we didn't; through a bad first marriage for her, a very tough illness for me, and on and on. Even though we now live a thousand miles away and have very different lives, one phone call and it's always like we've never spent a moment apart.

Stacy currently isn't hugely observant; she doesn't have two sets of dishes for keeping kosher, or stop her busy schedule because it's Shabbat. It's just that she is Jewish, celebrates Jewish holidays and has Jewish friends. Her family has a bit of everything now: Her sister and her family are Orthodox, her parents are Messianic, her grandmother is a Jehovah's Witness, and her brother is a JuBu: That's what you call someone who is Jewish and practices Buddhism. I think that's kind of clever. The point about Stacy's family is they all get together for major holidays and life cycle events (*Chanukah, Rosh Hashanah, Bar Mitzvahs, etc.*), and it works somehow. I respect that.

The wedding was beautiful and Stacy looked so pretty in her ivory satin gown and thick red hair under the veil. The rabbi (Reform) did a nice job as they all stood under the *chuppah*,[22] in the filtered light, while overhead trees had scattered the ground with their autumnal confetti of gold, russet, and brown. And when her husband broke the glass everyone cheered *Mazel Tov*[23] in unison. They walked back down the aisle as man and wife and little pleasantries began all around us: "Oh, such a lovely ceremony." "Didn't she

---

22 *The traditional wedding canopy representing both the home the couple will build together and God's covering in the marriage.*

23 *Congratulations. Another Jewish tradition is the groom to break a glass wrapped in a napkin. It has various meanings. One is that the marriage will last as long as the glass is shattered (forever), another is show joy even in the midst of our sorrow that the Temple was destroyed.*

look amazing?" "Isn't that weird cousin Edna over there?" "So, where's the bar?" At the reception, we all held hands and danced the *hora* in a large circle. At one point, the men formed an inner circle, lifting Stacy and her husband on chairs, high in the air, while they held a napkin between them. It's a traditional Jewish-wedding thing to do.

It was great.

And heartbreaking.

I intently tried to look happy and clap along. But it became one of those moments when time slows down, the music suddenly sounds far away, and people's faces get blurry. I shifted my weight and tilted my head, so my welled up tears didn't instantly gush down my checks. I didn't want Tim to see my sadness. Not to mention the fact that I had forgotten to use waterproof mascara so I figured if I angled my head back enough the black streaks going toward my ears might look more exotic than two racing stripes down my face.

See, we didn't have any of that at our wedding except the *chuppah*. Although, come to think of it, our vows were done outside too, but in early June when the grass and the leaves were bright green and summer was ahead of us. Now, looking back and being honest with myself, I knew the whole Jewish thing had mattered to me then but I couldn't construct a way to make it blend in my head. I told myself Tim isn't Jewish, and I want him so it doesn't matter. Then, as it still is now, aside from my immediate family, we just weren't a part of any Jewish community. Guess that big break with Messianic Judaism in my early teens had affected me more than I wanted to admit. Most of the people who attended our wedding were nice Christian *goyim*[24]. We're talking Jell-O molds, casseroles, gold-star stickers for good attendance at Sunday school, and sensible shoes. Communion at their churches is grape juice in tiny plastic cups and white bread cut up into squares. Now I ask you, what were *they* going to do if *Hava Nagila*[25] started to play?

I adored Tim and couldn't wait till we could get married and was looking forward to being part of his family. I craved the security and stability that his older, retired-Army parents instilled. My mother-in-law, whom I dearly love, is an honest-to-God real 1950's housewife, stopping just shy of vacuuming in pearls. Seriously. During our engagement I had the opportunity to privately show my mother and sister her oven. "Come 'ere. Ya gotta see this," I waved them over. We three peeked in. It was a showroom-immaculate twenty year-old oven. Ours was like us — splattered from years and years of our noisy bubbling celebrations and mom's odd recipes[26].

---

24 *Hebrew: non-Jews*

25 *Hebrew song that has become a staple at Jewish events, such as weddings, Bar and Bat Mitvahs.*

26 *She once made a strawberry and garlic salad. Don't ask.*

JEW IN THE PEW

So, although I have never regretted marrying Tim, I always wanted to be that radiant bride raised up on the chairs with my husband, while everyone danced around us. Just like Stacy. After her wedding, back at the hotel, I was washing my face and trying to get the mascara out of my ears when Tim called in from the other room, "You seemed a little upset tonight." I'm guessing he noticed the strange tilt of my head for most of the evening. This led into a big conversation and not a particularly pleasant one. He was afraid that I would reject him as part of my exploring this identity crisis of mine. Nonsense, I told him. Of all the things I'm not sure of in this world, he isn't one of them.

The next day we packed to fly back home. I'm worried that in the discomfort of our heavy talk, I might have forgotten to throw in the comfy shoes I have been wearing for years. Nah, couldn't be. I'll keep looking. What I am really afraid of is that in admitting how deeply I feel the need to be more Jewish, it might mean walking away from Christianity. I feel unmoored, adrift between crosscurrents... and shoeless.

The air is still, humid and motionless. I'm sitting outside watching Otis hunt lizards. Maybe I'm sick.

I woke up this morning feeling empty and lifeless inside. Let's face it; I don't have the energy for today's to-do list. I'm overwhelmed with all this religious evaluating introspective crap I've been doing. It seems like I'm marching off into the blurry unknown. Speaking of which, I still can't find those shoes.

Otis is now merrily trotting off with his prize; a green lifeless tail hangs from his mouth. Well, at least he is getting something done today. The lizard had probably been sitting on a rock, thinking about his life and now it's over. Maybe I should go take my temperature.

The phone is ringing... No, no Otis, I'll get it. You just keep rolling around on top of your dead lizard.

That was some nice church lady who just called, asking me to help out with something. "Sorry, I'd love to but my current bout with existentialism has left me in a malaise so I really can't commit." She seemed to take that well. You just have to be honest with people.

For a while there, I got busy doing stuff in church "for God," but it seriously chaffed, like corduroy on sunburn. The truth is that going to church has always felt un-me, like I need to run home to change my clothes into something that actually fits. And just like ignoring the fact that those jeans I've been wearing do nothing for my muffin-top, I have too long pretended that being unconnected to my Jewish culture and identity while doing the Gentile Christian thing it isn't a problem. I can't tell you how many times a well-meaning Christian has told me that I *just* need to find my identity in Christ. You mean, like I *just* need to

JEW IN THE PEW

lop off part of my body and the pants will fit? I know those people are just trying to be helpful. However, their comment shows their incomprehension of how hard it is to even be a believing Jew in a church. I don't want to worship Jesus the way they do, using words that have been used in association with a great deal of persecution (like "Christ" or "crusade"), ignore the biblical Feasts, or focus so heavily on the New Testament and sort of dismiss much of the *Tanakh*[27]. This reminds me of a song. In the 1970's an album came out called *Free to Be You and Me*[28] in which there was a song about helping:

And some kind of help is the kind of help
That helping's all about.
And some kind of help is the kind of help
We all can do without.

When I was a toddler and still lived in the country, our yellow lab Moby used to bring my mother presents, like dead rabbits. He was so sure that she felt about them like he did. So, it's always a bit of a lifeless

---

27 *The Tanach is the Torah, Prophets and Writings. The whole Hebrew Bible, a.k.a. the Old Testament.*

28 *It was produced by Marlo Thomas with the help of her famous friends to create an album of children's songs, stories and poems that illustrated that whether you were a boy or girl, you could become anything in life, not hemmed in by constraints of what you must do or look like or be. It was very forward thinking at the time when women were not yet commonly becoming doctors, lawyers or business managers.*

animal dropped at my feet when someone tells me who I am, "like as if" *they* know. It's a bad feeling when it comes from a fellow Jew – someone who should understand rejection based on who they are. But it's an even worse feeling when it comes from a Christian – a supposed spiritual sister or brother. Either way, it leaves me feeling defensive, misunderstood and, quite frankly, lonely. It's usually at this time Friendly Mr. Christian delivers his next gift, "Well, you converted so why should it matter?" Oy, such a statement.

Have I mentioned that I wasn't feeling well? My stomach is bothering me now. Calling me a convert is NOT okay. Number one, Jesus was a Jew. I realized some people tend to forget this, what with their pictures of him looking like He came from Scandinavia and all, but it's true. I'm not Jewish anymore why? — Because I happen to believe a certain first-century man was the one we had been waiting for? What difference does that make? I could worship the Lucky Charms cereal leprechaun if I wanted and still be a Jew. I did not convert to what was already mine — believing in the Jewish Messiah.

You know what is even weirder? A great deal of Christianity is based on, and taken from, Old Testament Judaism. Atonement for the forgiveness of sins, that perpetual light in the sanctuary, singing psalms in worship, the Ten Commandments, and even being raised from the dead and eternal life, etc., are all part of Jewish thought. But, what was once set up by

JEW IN THE PEW

God is now so far removed from its roots that even a believing Jew feels alienated. Forget how a Jew would feel if he wasn't already of the believing persuasion.

So, I admit it, although I love God, at church I often feel terrible and can't wait till it's over. And lately I've found myself becoming more disinterested in all things Christian. At the same time, hungrily reading more about the Jewish traditions that I hardly get to put into practice. This feels wrong in the Christian part of me and yet interested, happy, and proud in the Jewish part. Well, thank God, at least I'm not conflicted in all this — that can make a person sick. I should really count my blessings seeing that Otis doesn't bring me any dead animals either. He keeps his lizards to himself.

6
THE START OF THE SEASON

"IT WAS ONE OF THOSE PERFECT ENGLISH AUTUMNAL DAYS WHICH OCCUR MORE FREQUENTLY IN MEMORY THAN IN LIFE."
— P.D. JAMES

Walking through the Farmer's Market, I stop by Maggie's Herb Farm stall. The smell of the fresh dill suddenly mutes all busyness around me and I'm in my grandmother's kitchen as a little girl watching her make chicken soup.

I re-juggle the bags in my hands so I can get to my cell phone. "Hi Gra! Can ya hear me? Uh oh..." Then, in a moment of real sophistication, with my phone wedged between my shoulder and ear, I try to catch a runaway onion just as the wind blinds me with my own hair. I try to whip my head around in what I thought would be like those Sports Illustrated models coming out of the surf — instead I bang myself in the head with my reusable cloth bag that's holding a jar of local honey. "Oh man, that hurt! Gra? Gra? You still there?" Honey is now oozing past my eye with a nice patch of hair stuck to it.

I want to know what my grandmother, who is now 89, remembered about *Rosh Hashanah* and the holidays from when she was a child. She was happy to go on a trip down memory lane; "The first thing that got you was the delicious smell when you walked in the door. It was unbelievable!" Her mother, Jenny, after whom I'm named, had five daughters and one son, and was a real *balabusta*[29]. When they all started getting married and having children my great-grandfather made long benches so at the holidays everyone could sit together down a row of tables for brisket and kasha and *tsimmes*[30], chicken soup with matzo balls, gefilte fish and horseradish and challah. I wish I could have been to one of those *Rosh Hashanah* meals, standing next to Gramom Jenny as she rolled the matzo balls. She died before I knew her[31].

---

29 *Yiddish for superb homemaker.*
30 *A yummy casserole of carrots and sweet potatoes, stewed with honey and possibly dried fruits.*
31 *Gra's mother was born in Russia in the late nineteenth century. Like so many Eastern European Jews of that time,*

THE START OF THE SEASON

While Gra talked, I could hear the old Russian Yiddish accents and the bustle of getting ready; the clinking pots and dishes being set out; the sounds of benches moved on a wood floor; the steam coming off the soup carried the sounds of little irritations with one another, laughter, and gossip, down the hall and over the table. "Gra, do ya think..." I asked while licking the honey off my finger, "...our kids really get the fact that when we celebrate a Jewish holiday we are part of this long line of thousands of family members that came before us?" I ask as I drove home, phone still clutched between check and shoulder as I keep wiping off my sticky forehead. The pot of dill is belted in the seat next to me. Hopefully, I can get it home without spilling dirt all over the car[32]. Her answer was a little less validating then what I wanted, "Yeah. Why not? Sure they get it. When are you coming to visit?"

Walking in the house, I toss my keys on the chest of drawers by the front door. They skitter towards a gold framed old black and white picture of Gramom Jenny, Grampop Harry, all their adult kids with their spouses and the next generation, which was my mother's. Mom is perched up on a piano, looking like she feels pretty special with her little seven year old

---

they packed up their few belongings and boarded a boat in a world of persecution, to go to a land in a world of freedom.

32 *Not like that time I bought 25 little goldfish for our pond, slammed on the breaks and the bag broke open. There was a carpool ride, we will never forget.*

legs dangling down. I thought of what Gra's piano looked like when I was younger. It was covered with framed pictures, some of which I now have. Around this time of year it would display *Rosh Hashanah* cards from my grandmother's siblings and their families and lots of friends. I'd thoughtfully leaf through them. Then, as a teenager, I felt their absence — that part of my extended Jewish family with whom I was no longer connected. My grandmother still talked to them occasionally, and heard about their family events. But the contact pretty much stopped there. It didn't make sense to me that the fact we believed Yeshua was the Messiah and still did Jewish things like celebrate the holidays meant such division among relatives. I wouldn't cut a loved one out of my life because they believed in Zoastrianism, or Hinduism or any "ism" for that matter. What does that have to do with being family and loving each other? I can't imagine what that must have been like for my mother, who had always been close to her aunts and cousins. I wish I could reconnect with them all now, but I'm not sure that's possible.

"When life gives you a problem, plant or cook something." I just made that quote up. Pretty good, don't you think? I can't fix the fact that we are removed from our extended family by 900 miles, a couple of decades and a perceived religious divide. I can, however, make sure that my kids have positive holiday memories with their grandmothers (Mom and

THE START OF THE SEASON

Gra), aunt (Ellen) and cousins (El's kids) and find some ways to reinforce their Jewish identity. But first I'm going to plant the dill so there will be some to snip when I make chicken soup next week and then go take a shower. Honey is still in my hair.

Tim is making waffles in the kitchen, the kids are nearby watching TV. I've got a cup of coffee and the newspaper in front of me, with Otis by my side.

The Jacksonville Jewish News comes once a month. There is a pretty active Jewish community there. It is an hour away so it's not like the events listed are around the corner. Usually, I read the paper with longing. Then sigh, fold the paper, feel melancholy and return to my regularly scheduled life. But, that's just it, isn't it? I don't want what has been *status quo* around here. As I skim over articles and announcements, an inchoate thought emerges. Not wanting to disrupt this gestating idea, I pick up my mug and give myself a little space from the noise of the big open living room-kitchen area. The dining room is set off a bit and there our big table serves as my project area.

Rearranging my piles of photos and papers that will become a scrapbook one day, I start asking myself questions. "Okay, what if things weren't so far away, would you go?" "What do you want to go to and why?" "Why feel this way and do nothing?" "What are you afraid of?" What a good shrink I'd make. I should give myself $75.

By the time my coffee is cold and the table is organized, I've gotten some clarity like a ship sailing in out of the mist. I now see that all the reasons for not participating in a Jewish community all this time had less to do with my location or about Tim. It had to do with me. All these years *I've* been the one telling me that I wasn't allowed to join in. No one else has been saying that to me. I have been waiting for a stamp of approval in some way, a permission slip to play with others. But that isn't reality. I'm Jewish, dammit, so I'm in. I don't have to go along with this outdated notion that because I believe Yeshua is the Messiah I am some sort of Jewish reject. Ok, yes, there have been some very painful instances of abandonment in my life. But *I* get to choose what they mean. At some point in the past, I decided who would and who wouldn't reject me and where I could and could not go. No more. This is where Rosa Parks decides she can sit wherever she damn well pleases. It just doesn't have to matter what kind of Jew I am.

With my recent epiphany I go back to the newspaper on the coffee table in the living room. Little does my family realize what a monumental shift has just occurred in my psyche. I try to nonchalantly read the paper again. Sometimes you just have to sit

THE START OF THE SEASON

on a moment and not blab out loud all your profound and earth shattering thoughts at once. I've found that doing so can drain those around you. Odd but true.

It's then I see it, an event for tomorrow.

I yelled into the kitchen, "Hey, wanna go to a *shofar*[33] making event?" Tim's getting eggs and milk from inside the fridge and bending down to pull things out of cabinets. "A what?" and he starts clattering something else. Tim grew up with his dad making waffles every weekend and so Tim *loves* to make waffles. I'm not saying it's on par with my angst about our continuity, or lack thereof, but he feels very strongly about them. I try to make myself heard over the noise of the TV and the mixer, "TO MAKE A SHOF..." He stops the mixer that makes it apparent that I've been yelling.

All three kids look at me — our two and Ellen's youngest, my niece Libi, who slept over last night. Tim continues to oil the griddle and pour batter as I explain. "It should be fun. We'll go and make our own shofar. It says here that you pay $5 and pick out a ram's horn and then are taught how to drill and finish it. So this year at *Rosh Hashanah* you can each have your own to blow!" They turn back to the TV. Otis

---

33 *Shofar is a ritual instrument made from a ram's horn that is used for Jewish religious purposes, most often during Rosh Hashanah and Yom Kippur. Though in the days before phones, Israel was called to move or to gather by various shofar blasts.*

gives a little snort and stretches in a new direction. Tim turns the waffle maker over, takes a moment to study my face and says, "Mom's right, guys, it'll be fun. We're going to go."

Woohoo! I pick up the phone to call Ellen and tell her what our plans are for tomorrow. She can meet us there and pick up Libi. And I just got to tell her about my latest revelation. So much for keeping deep thoughts to myself for a while. I think I'll celebrate with a waffle or two.

Just back from a walk on the beach and feeling surprisingly optimistic. Today's quote: "The weak can never forgive. Forgiveness is the attribute of the strong." – Mahatma Gandhi.

I feel sooo much better! I didn't even realize how much that hurt had been weighing me down. I wonder if I'm taller now than my usual 5 foot 3. The ten days between *Rosh Hashanah (which is both the Jewish New Year and the Feast of Trumpets)* and *Yom Kippur (The Day of Atonement)* are called the *Days of Awe*. This is a time of introspection, of examining the past year and of reconciling with anyone you have offended, sinned against or even wronged inadvertently. It's about your relationship with God, with others, and even with yourself.

THE START OF THE SEASON

At the Shofar making class the other day — a fun activity except we all came home smelling like sheep — the rabbi mentioned doing *Tashlikh*, something I wasn't familiar with. So I did some reading. *Tashlikh* is Hebrew for "casting off" and it's doing something in the physical to represent something in the spiritual. It works like this: You go to a flowing body of water — such as the ocean, a creek, a river, or possibly in a pinch you could use a fish tank with a recirculating pump — and empty your pockets of small pieces of bread or crumbs, metaphorically casting off your sins. Micah 7:18-20 is recited and sometimes people sing and worship afterwards, as well.

When I read about this practice, a certain rather hurtful person's name sprang to mind. I really didn't want to forgive her. I was totally justified in my entrenched resentment but you know how it is with conviction, you've just got to heed the call. Leaving a disappointed Otis at home, I headed to the beach alone to practice my own *Tashlikh*. I decided to use a rock, though, instead of breadcrumbs because it was a big issue in my life, and I thought the situation deserved something with a bit more heft. With a marker, I wrote all over the stone my feelings of betrayal, pain and anger. I asked God to forgive me for my bitterness toward this person, and for actively holding onto the pain. With that, I hurled the rock, with its transferred pain, into the sea.

JEW IN THE PEW

Now, let me just interject here that, although I have some impressive biceps, I throw like a girl. Many a time my kids have asked me to toss them something like the remote, an apple or something only to find themselves diving for cover or double over in laughter after I failed to hit the target by 6 feet. So, right as the rock left my hand, I thought, "Oh, no! How lame is that to have to retrieve your sin-laden rock in the sand because you missed *the ocean*!" Thank God, though, it plunked into the water. I felt refreshed, my hurt and anger had been successfully tossed into the watery abyss. I'm so glad I didn't use breadcrumbs. Watching little bits of a *challah* or *ciabatta* become a soggy floating mess wouldn't have felt nearly as a profound an act of spiritual cleansing.

So with newfound lightness I glided on home grateful for the ability to give my sin to God and my heritage to have provided such a lovely symbolic act.

L'shanah Tovah![34] *Rosh Hashanah and the Fall Jewish holidays is a time for family dinners, synagogue services and spiritual accounting. It always has a festive feel. Today we had a big meal with Mom, Gra, El, and all the*

---

[34] *Hebrew: A good year for you! A common Rosh Hashanah New Year's Greeting*

THE START OF THE SEASON

kids at three o'clock and I tried out some new recipes. Note to self: The dates stuffed with goat cheese is not a keeper.

Earlier this morning, we went to church and then I came home to finish cooking. The most upsetting time to be a Jew in a church is during a Jewish holiday because barely anyone but you knows it. I don't hear a "Happy *Rosh Hashanah*" or even a Hebrew or Yiddish holiday greetings of *L'shanah Tovah, Chag Semeach.*[35] It makes me sad. Not only because the lack of mention from pulpit or friend is a true indicator that I am culturally out of sync. It also makes me sad because Rosh Hashanah, like the other holidays coming up, are in *their* Bible and yet deemed irrelevant. If you went to synagogue on this day, you would be all dressed up. There would be a holiday feel in the air, as people greet each other with any of the aforementioned salutations. It's like the way people joyfully greet one another at Christmas Eve services at church: even those they don't know.

Now, to see it from where I am standing, picture you are Joe Christian and it's Christmas. You walk into what is supposed to be your faith community, but you are the only one who even knows what day it is. There are no cards, no holiday spirit, no mention in the service, no one hugs you and says "Happy Holidays." You mention the lack to someone in charge and they

---

35 *Hebrew: for a good year or joyous holiday*

JEW IN THE PEW

look at you blankly, and then dismissively try to assure you that God doesn't care about that anymore.

So you can imagine why I hate going to church during the Jewish holidays. Needless to say, I just went to church this morning for Tim and the kids. It means a lot to them that I am there and for it to be a family thing. Though let's be honest, Mommy felt empty and sat or stood by rote without emotion or interest. I was grateful for the 20-minute ride home, where I said nothing, but stared out the passenger side window waiting for my true self to restart. As the overhanging trees, with dripping Spanish moss, and gated communities gave way to yawning stretches of hammock, sand and sea, I felt better. I was eager to get home, shake off my negative feelings about church, and get back into the holiday spirit by finishing up setting the table and our meal preparations, because the family was coming over soon.

Things are supposed to be sweet on *Rosh Hashanah* to symbolize a sweet New Year. Apples and honey are traditional, as are glazed carrots that are cut into rounds, like coins, to symbolize wealth for the coming year. I almost forgot and put the salt on the table by habit. You aren't supposed to have anything salty or bitter on the *Rosh Hashanah* menu. Think of it this way: You are a people with a long history of the world always plotting against you, be it Holocaust, Pogrom,

THE START OF THE SEASON

Inquisition, Crusades or just a horde of Philistines with glandular problems. Having a dinner table laden with only the sweet is a nice expression of hope for the year to come.

The chicken soup with matzo balls was delicious. The brisket came out of the oven so tender it was falling apart, coated in thick, glossy gravy. Ellen brought the *kugel*[36] and the *kasha*[37]. Sometimes, I find it funny when we eat our traditional Jew food in sunny Florida, because we are really just eating 19th century peasant food from the old country of Eastern Europe. After all, that is where most American Jews came from, my family included.

The table looked gorgeous, and we all had a nice feast and family time: talking at once, over-eating, prying into each other's lives, reaching across the table, sprinkling the evening with quips and laughter. However, I forgot the round *Challah*. It's braided egg bread made for Shabbat or holidays. It is generally oblong shaped, but on *Rosh Hashanah*, it is round and sweet to symbolize that the coming year will roll around smoothly without any sorrow. I just got so busy cooking and getting ready, I didn't leave myself enough time to go buy one or make one. I guess that's okay. I mean, forgetting the bread should be my greatest problem, right? After dinner, with the crumbs still on

---

36 *Yiddish: noodle pudding*
37 *Buckwheat groats.*

JEW IN THE PEW

the tablecloth and the almost empty glasses scattered around, I pushed my distended belly full of brisket and kugel away from the table; and I wondered what this year would hold, since I was finally being honest with myself and trying to make changes.

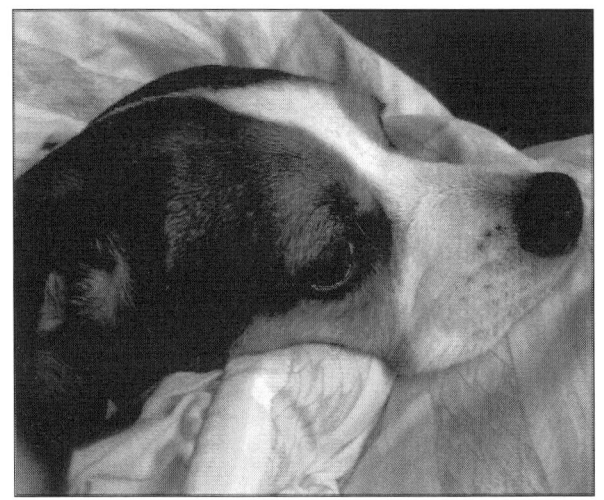

Otis

7
RESEARCH

"HE WHO WOULD SEARCH FOR PEARLS MUST DIVE BELOW."
— JOHN DRYDEN

It's been raining for days.
It's warm and damp; a recipe for mildew. Nothing says good
things are a-coming like rotten weather.

This climate is doing nothing for my hair. I've been doing the straight blown out look but with this weather I might as well give that up. All this humidity is returning my hair back to its original tousled sort of waviness. And just as I have been wrestling with my hair, I've been toying with the idea of going to synagogue on *Yom Kippur*. The white noise of the blow dryer makes it a good time to think. In the past, the idea of going into a synagogue kind of freaked me out. I was sure they would all stand up and turn on me because I am a believer that somehow they would instantly know just by looking at me. It's not as if I would walk in with a huge crucifix swaying and thumping against my chest while wearing a "Got Jesus?" t-shirt, and punctuating my sentences with a hearty "Thank you, Jeeezus."

Trying to find the right hair product under the sink, I give a big sigh. The noise echoes off the bathroom walls and sounds louder than it should be. Of course, the obvious answer would be to go to a *Messianic* congregation. Yeah, well, I would but the closest one is over an hour away. Besides I popped in there once to check it out and something didn't sit right with me, though I couldn't put my finger on it. I strongly felt that it was not the right place for me, even if I lived next door, and that's all I'm going to say. So only churches surround me. It seems to me that my option for this Jew, who decided Jesus is the Messiah, is to go to church, and do it the Gentile way. What a drag.

RESEARCH

As I brush my hair, the rain starts to come down harder and the thought pops up, "Maybe I shouldn't straddle both worlds, if the Jewish aspect is so important to me." The idea is so surprising that I just stare in the mirror, my hairbrush paused in midair. One pair of my brown eyes fixed on another, I notice the dark rings around my irises and ask myself, "How attached am I to being a Christian? Why not be just one or the other?"

I went downstairs; letting the concept, and the reality of such a decision, roll around in my head like two cue balls alternately clacking together, and then rolling apart. I folded laundry and thought. I worked on an article and thought. I took Otis for a rainy walk and thought under the umbrella. I started making Chicken Piccata and pounded the cutlets and thought. To even consider walking away from a faith which your life has revolved around for decades is profoundly stressful.

I had my answer at the same time I realized that I had turned our cutlets into a gross raw mash. One, it was God who made me a Jew in the first place. And, two, I cannot turn my back on who I truly believe is the One everybody is waiting for. Nor do I want to. It's just really unfair that Yeshua has been cloaked in so much Gentile culture for the last two millennia that now I stand here struggling to find a way to stay connected to the very thing a spiritually-driven kind of Jew wants — *their* Messiah. Also altered beyond its original state, as is tonight's chicken.

JEW IN THE PEW

Out come the cookbooks, I need to a recipe that calls for the texture of what I now have in front of me. I'm not going to throw away almost perfectly good meat. Don't get me wrong; there is much of Christian culture that I do like and respect. It's not all *goishe drek*[38]. I really enjoy a great sermon that is full of hard-hitting questions that make me think, challenges me, and teaches me things I don't know. I love times of worship that are tender and intimate. I need those grounding moments with God to calm my mental gerbil-on-the-wheel tendency.

Women's Bible study is another plus. Sitting with a small group of women who are willing to bare their souls, dig deep to find more of what God has for us, and support each other, while we laugh and cry over our lives, is great. I have probably done almost every Beth Moore Bible study she's written (Beth, btw, if you are reading this — we need to do lunch). But as much as I enjoy and look forward to all these things, it doesn't offset my desire to be with Jewish people, and to want Jewish things in my life. It comes up in Bible study, in worship, in sermons, at holidays, and even in times of just fellowship. I try not to let it feel like a big deal, but truthfully, it feels like banging yourself in a place where you already have a bruise. So now I have two questions to ask myself: how long can I stay in a

---

38 *Yiddish. Meaning shoddy or inferior non-Jewish merchandise.*

RESEARCH

place where I continually feel so out of place, and what am I going to do about dinner?

Books and papers are all over my desk. Bills are waiting to be paid, field trip permission slips are waiting to be signed and an article is waiting to be started. I ignore all that to search the web instead.

I love googling the answers to questions that routinely punctuate my day, like: How come that muscle is called your trapezius? What is a good substitute to use when you run out of vinegar? Isn't there an app for predicting which irrational mood will surface when I'm PMS-ing? I really should be reconciling our checking account, the bills are piling up and if I don't track down that letter from Zander's teacher, I'm in real trouble. I know it's in this pile somewhere. Do you have any idea what a failure you feel like when all the other kids' moms remembered to bring in the right thing on the right day for whatever non-educational-lets-give-overwhelmed-parents-one-more-stupid-thing-to-do that was planned?

So instead of attending to said urgent needs, I'm on the internet looking up *Yom Kippur*. Usually you have to buy tickets for High Holiday services weeks in advance. It's a whole big deal. Churches throw their doors wide open to those in spiritual need, especially on a major holiday. But in almost every synagogue it is the opposite; the holiest day of the year, and you need to pay for a ticket to get in. A pretty hefty price too — think Broadway or airfare — which is just ridiculous. I mean, really, so why should we pay to pray with our own people, to our own God? Okay, okay, I know why.

Churches support themselves by passing the plate during services but this is not done in synagogues. Jewish law prohibits handling money on Shabbat and on holidays. Still the rabbi needs to make a living, the electric bill needs to be paid, and the building needs to be paid for so instead there are membership dues and ticket sales. There is a debate going on about this practice and if it should continue. The pro side says that the ticket price for High Holiday services help keep the synagogue running and without which they would go under. Those in the other camp say that it discourages outreach, which is exactly what Judaism in America needs to do to attract the next generation to synagogue.

All I know if that I want to do something this *Yom Kippur* and I'm just not going to plunk down a car payment to do it. Feeling indignant I abruptly shove my chair away from my desk to go find something to eat. This sudden move startles Otis who has taken his rightful place in the big white wicker chair next to my desk. He takes his job very seriously. When it's time for me to write, it's time for him to sit nearby in case I need him. Frankly, I wish he would contribute a little more than moral support but at least he's there to vent to. "Otis, relax. I'm just going to the kitchen." He is still looking at me so I explain about having to buy tickets for services and how *fakakta*[39] that is. He heaves a sigh and gives the canine equivalent to the shrug, palms up, "What can you do?" and goes back to sleep.

While ingesting 500 calories that I doubt I'm ever going to work off, and shaking my keyboard to get the crumbs out, I stare out the window for a minute. Otis is gently snoring. The grandfather clock is ticking away in the foyer to the left off my office. The mailman is making his way around the cul-de-sac — a metal mailbox door slaps shut, the "grrrr" of his boxy little truck advances 100 feet, another mailbox slaps shut, another 100 feet...

There must be a synagogue somewhere open to visitors for the High Holy Days. I really feel drawn to go. I can't even remember the last time I attended a *Yom Kippur* service. How bad is that! Many Jews who are unobservant the rest of the year get themselves to *shul*[40] for *Yom Kippur*. I am, once again, awash in a wave of Bad-Jew guilt – it kind of feels like indigestion. You know Christmas/Easter Christians? Well, the Jewish equivalent is a *Yom Kippur* Jew – you, at least, show up for the biggies. I suppose that I could pretend *Yom Kippur* is like any other day and stay in the oblivious

---

39 *Yiddish for crappy, screwed up, etc.*
40 *Yiddish: synagogue*

Christian part of my world. I have done that in the past. Though, honestly, I was always pretty bitchy on those days, what with the guilt and feelings of isolation percolating through me, and all.

A breeze from the open window ruffles all the papers around me. I better get to work. I begin to make piles — books go here, bills go there, interview notes go to my right, school stuff goes in the trash (just kidding) — until I can see my desk once again. I wish I could compartmentalize my feelings as easily as I can with my desk. Unfortunately, I can't. My sister though is great at it, which does seem a little unfair. Well, that and the fact that she got the better hair.

8
YOM KIPPUR

"Courage is resistance to fear, not the absence of fear" — Mark Twain

It's one of those days when I just want to stay in yoga pants and a t-shirt. No makeup, no hair done.
Feeling a little dismantled.

I wouldn't have even gone to church this morning except a buddy of ours was preaching. The more honest I am with myself about this whole issue, the harder it is to go to church. But, out of deference to my sweet husband, our friend and our kids, I hauled myself out of bed, pulled on some clothes, carefully pasted on the Everything's Fine Mask, and went.

We greeted people on the way in, "Oh, hi. Yes, fine. You?" and sat down in our usual spot, off to the right,

JEW IN THE PEW

slightly forward of center, on the isle. I was looking through the bulletin which barely ever changes when a pleasant lady whose name I never recall stopped by to tell me she enjoys having Emme in Sunday School, "She's always involved in the discussion and shares her opinions!" Hmm, I'm sure she does, being the chip off the block here. The music begins; everyone stands and starts to sing. Except me. My mask is slipping and I can just feel my moody contemplation showing.

Before long it was sermon time — my favorite part of the service being the writer and information junkie that I am — but I really couldn't focus. The only thing I heard Sean say was, "It is a virtual impossibility to act in a way inconsistent with how we think of ourselves." I quickly wrote it down and then promptly veered off in thought as he went on with what was probably a great sermon. How we think of ourselves, huh? Maybe that's it. Maybe I am unsure of how I view myself. Jewish or Christian? I wish it wasn't an odd thing to be Jewish *and* a Christian. It really shouldn't be. Jesus was. The disciples were. Thousands and thousands of first-century followers were. Okay, actually there was no Christianity then; it was the Jewish Messiah and those who believed in Him. All the major players in the Bible celebrated the Feasts of the Lord. If you think about it, it's kind of odd Christians don't recognize *Yom Kippur* on any level since atoning for sin is such a big part of their vernacular. Doesn't being a Christian

YOM KIPPUR

mean you want to do things that Jesus did, at least, like discussing the holidays that where important to Him?

I vaguely registered that the service had moved on to the communal recitation of the Nicene Creed, that 1700-year-old declaration that Yeshua was with God from the beginning. As the congregation droned on, I thought about "God from God, Light from Light, being of one substance with the Father..." It's confuses me why Christianity separates it all so much because when God gave Moses the instructions about the Day of Atonement, Jesus as the Word of God was there, just as they say.

The front rows got up and formed a line, making their way to the rail to receive communion. Then the next row, and so on. People kneel down, palms out stretched for starched little wafers that resemble a patch of dry wall. Ironically, my stomach grumbled. The line edges closer towards us, which I saw but was daydreaming of a *Yom Kippur* long ago. Jerusalem would have had the holiday bustle, everyone busy getting ready for a High Holy Day. What was it like for Jesus on those days, looking at faces of those he came to save, hearing the sacrificial sheep baying bleating from their pens, and smelling the scent of blood coming from the Temple courtyards.

Was He pensive each *Yom Kippur* knowing He was the ultimate atonement?

Did He think back to that day in the Sinai when this was all set in motion?

Was He expectant, eager to stand in the gap and close the distance between man and God?

Someone to my left gestures it's my turn to go up front. I shake my head, move my legs to the side and wave them past me. Jolted out of my reverie, the pang of having an experience different than everyone else is the room twangs anew. On one hand, I am overcome with feelings of gratitude about Yeshua's connection to *Yom Kippur*. On the other hand, I feel so sad and confused that I am unable to share these emotions with my faith community, because they believe that *Yom Kippur* has no validity as a Christian observance... of any kind.

After church I quickly changed into the clothes I originally wanted to wear, tied my hair in a ponytail, and warmed up some leftover quiche. Tim and the kids all went their separate ways — the garage, a friend's house, upstairs to talk on the phone.

I let Otis out back where he went to lay down in the sun, content and happy with himself, his surroundings and, I'm guessing, his spiritual identity.

Following his lead I go outside too, bringing to the wrought iron table my plate and the Jacksonville Jewish News that came in the mail yesterday. My morning at church already seems a world away. I found an open invitation from a local Conservative synagogue for their *Yom Kippur* services, I try picturing going to these services. Maybe I could just slide in the back of the synagogue… maybe that would feel good… maybe I would feel at home.

I'm in the middle of a book about Jewish holidays and traditions, when the doorbell rings.

"Thanks Ray!" I holler out the front door as I bring in my latest shipment. I've seen a lot of the UPS guy lately. At least once a week he hops out of his truck and bounds up to the house. In one motion, he rings the bell and drops off an Amazon.com box before leaping back in the driver's seat and rumbling off. Those guys must really burn a lot of calories. Do they hire them based on aerobic stamina? I'd be terrible at that job. For one thing, I'm not much of a sprinter. But on the other hand I do look really good in brown.

I opened the package, put the newly arrived book on the growing stack in my office and headed back to living room to finish reading how *Yom Kippur* went from what we read in the Bible to today's observance. When the Romans destroyed the Temple in 70 A.D. the rabbis could no longer perform the ritual sacrifice on the Day of Atonement. So, instead, they decided that each individual should fast and focus on his or her indebtedness to God. All day is spent in synagogue, reciting prayers that admit our weakness and sin to God, while asking for His mercy. You fast from *Erev*[41] *Yom Kippur* through the next day at sundown when you get together with family or friends to "break the fast."

Just when I'm thinking about how I can't go longer than four or five hours without food, lest I get one helluva headache, the phone rings. It's Ellen. "Hey El, did ya ever think about why we always break the fast with bagels and lox?" Her erudite answer: "Because we do. That's all. So, anyway..." and then she went back to her original reason for calling. Right, thanks. I guess I could have asked my brother, but lately he hasn't even been returning my emails for some reason.

It turns out that although many families take the bagel and Lox route, though there are number of them that break the fast with a nice cocktail. I'm starting to think that might not be such a bad idea after all.

Yom Kippur. 7:00 PM. A pumpkin-scented candle flickers on the coffee table where the kids are doing their homework. Tim is on the phone with the cable company because they are over charging us. And I have a sink full of dirty dishes.

I went to that synagogue today for *Yom Kippur* services and can't stop thinking about it. I felt so

---

41 *Hebrew: meaning sundown the night of or night before.*

YOM KIPPUR

welcomed, loved hearing the Hebrew, seeing all the Jewish faces, and watching people greet one another with hugs and *Gut Yuntifs*[42]. It's a pretty serious service but like a dope I just sat there smiling.

Their building is beautiful. It was built in the 1920's. All the surrounding windows are stained glass, depicting biblical scenes: Adam in the garden, Noah and the ark, Moses at the burning bush, David killing Goliath. The crystal chandelier hanging from the two-story ceiling bounced light off the white walls. The wooden seats were dark and worn silky with use.

I sat down in the back, next to the sweetest little old lady with white hair, and the most amazing false eyelashes. It looked as if she glued them on in the 50's, and they have been there ever since. They were so pendulous; I don't know how she blinked. Lillian. That was her name. She introduced herself and asked about me, because she hadn't seen me before. I said I'm Jewish but my husband isn't, and we go to a church; but I really need some *yiddishkeit*[43] in my life right now. She patted my hand, blinked slowly and said, "I understand, my dear." Her acceptance melted me. I just might have poured out my whole heart to her at that moment if not for the fact that the cantor was singing just then.

Further into the service, I leaned over and asked her if she thought I would be welcome there; after

---

42 *Yiddish: Good Holiday*
43 *Yiddish: meaning things Yiddish or Jewish.*

all, I had previously admitted to going to church. To be honest, I *might* have made it out to sound a tad like that was my husband's fault, and not because I actually believe in Jesus. Though I don't think I was disavowing anything. Seriously, how much could I have explained at that moment? Lillian said not to worry because her husband wasn't Jewish either. He converted and they raised their son, who had recently died, in this synagogue. She said she couldn't talk about it because she might start crying. How sad. Besides that, what would happen to those eyelashes? I wondered what happened to her son, and turned my attention back to the service.

The prayers were so soothing, especially the *Vidui*, the confession. It is such a powerful and cleansing thing to stand with a group of individuals and, as one person, admit our sins before God. You know, even the best of us don't always remember or take ownership of our missteps. So centuries ago the rabbis created a long list of every mistake or sin they could think of – arranged alphabetically of course — which the congregation recites together. It's like the "Father, forgive us for what we have done and left undone" prayer before Communion in many churches, but ramped up like a hundred notches. It really covers all the bases, not just what we can remember at that particular moment. And it's always recited corporately, because we have communal responsibility for one another as a body, as a family, and as a people, which I think is a profound statement in and of itself.

YOM KIPPUR

As I stood, reciting these words that rabbis long ago put together to try to make things right between God, and us I felt something almost tangible inside. It was as if my gut was not crowded with organs and bones but a hollow space filled with dark liquid and as we went through the liturgy of repentance a swirl of new color began from a pin-point in the center and then stirring and swirling outward. It lightened the entire area and left me with an unusual sense of calm. I must admit that it was a deeply spiritual and healing moment to recite the *Vidui* then and there standing, alongside brothers and sisters with whom I only have in common that we are all Jews, publicly admitting failures and asking God for forgiveness.

After about two hours I had to go, my carriage was about to turn back into a pumpkin. I was about to scoot out the door when Lillian asked me to come back at six to break the fast. I felt bad telling her that I just might do that when I knew that I really wouldn't. I needed to return home and take care of my family. I felt a little like Cinderella rushing out the door before the clock stuck twelve.

At our dinner table tonight there are just the four of us, since the rest of my family cannot get together until tomorrow; and that warm *yiddishkeit* feeling I had earlier today was completely evaporated. I tried to tell Tim and the kids about the synagogue, the service, how beautiful and special it was, but they couldn't relate. Instead they rushed through a perfunctory

JEW IN THE PEW

dinner, took their plates to the sink and moved on to other things, like homework and the cable bill, just like it was any other day... and not something special, not something so full of continuity with your people... not something God ordained... just a regular old day.

But it wasn't. Not for me, at least. And I'm glad I went.

It's late afternoon. I'm laying down on the swing hanging from the Live Oak in the back yard. Pillow behind my head, book laid open across my chest staring up into the dappled sunlight through the leaves.

These trees here are far different from those up North. They're sculptural, twisted draping branches that dip and sway with the wind off the ocean. This variant of oaks is able to weather storms that would uproot their less pliant and more vertical cousins above the Mason-Dixon Line. I notice a deep gash in the bark on the limb above me. Something must have happened a long time ago to cause that. I've come out back to read under the trees and reorient myself. But I'm not sure it's working. One line in my book, "Only grieving can heal grief,[44]" and I'm back to thinking about breakfast. We went to Mom's the next day for

---

44 *Quote by Ann Lamott*

a huge bagels and lox, post-post *Yom Kippur* meal. I seriously overate and got a headache. But I doubt it's just indigestion that's upset me.

I begin to replay the morning in my head. We had all been sitting around, eating and talking. The usual thing, everyone talking at once, with six different conversations going on, while the food is being passed about the table. "Hey, can someone pass the lox over here?" "Really, she said that?" "What going on? Who are you talking about?" "No, I said it to Vera not Elsie." "She's talking about her phone conversation yesterday." "Oh, that's nice. Pass me the onions, will ya?" "Will somebody please hand me the lox down here! I'm never gonna get this bagel made. Hello? The lox!" Just a normal, calm family gathering. So, at one point I proudly mention to the table that I went to synagogue on *Yom Kippur*.

Silence. Heads turned in my direction; forks were suspended midair with onion rings or pieces of lox left dangling. It was brief, but silence nonetheless, a deafening occurrence in the midst of generations of non-stop talkers. "You did what?" "You really went?" "I wanted to do that but…" "Where did you go?" "Did you have to buy a ticket?" "Will ya shut up and let her talk!"

I told them about the Conservative synagogue where I didn't have to buy a ticket, how I met Lillian and how good it felt. My mother fires a question across the table like a gun off the bow of a ship, "Yeah, and

JEW IN THE PEW

what do you think they are going to do when they find out you are a Messianic Jew?" Startled by the tone and the question, I look up from my plate and take in her raised eyebrows, pursed lips, flared nostrils. I had expected my family would have been supportive.

Within moments I am on the defensive, feeling my shoulders square and hearing my voice get that bellow-y back off edge: "Look, I am really missing some *yiddishkeit*, ya know? And I wanted to go. Besides, I hardly think someone is gonna run up to me and ask me point blank if Jesus Christ is my Lord and Savior!"

At that point my sister, always the mediator, pours herself some more coffee and says: "I think things are different now. It's not like it was years ago, and maybe now people aren't so uptight about it all." She reaches across the table for the sweetener and continues, "After all, with all the interfaith marriages there is a lot more tolerance."

The kid's sense something afoot and are assembling and eating their bagels with unusual attentiveness. I give Ellen a grateful smile from across the table but try to hold my ground. "Well, Tim isn't Jewish so technically we are an interfaith family. And saying what I did to Lillian *does not* disown my belief that Yeshua is the Messiah." Which is what I assumed Mom was worried about. After this went round the table for a while, I finally turn back to my mother. "Mah, why dontcha understand what I am saying!? I

YOM KIPPUR

miss Jewish things. That's all." All of a sudden she looks forlorn. Softly she says, "I understand, Jenn. I understand," and quietly goes off to the kitchen.

The usual commotion of clanking plates and multiple conversations resumed along the table. Tim and my brother-in-law start talking about business; obviously relieved this charged thing between the women in the family has ended. But I sat there breathing shallowly, focused intently on placing capers and onions on my bagel.

Gee, you think I might get a headache after that? Sensing my mood, Otis just popped up on the swing with me. He takes his job of being a comforter very seriously. I reposition him because his paw is digging into my solar plexus and lay back down. We rock back and forth and again I notice that scar in the tree. Now that I think about it, I feel really bad for my mother. For years, she had been very involved in her synagogue but as soon as the news went out that she had believed in Yeshua, her synagogue friends never called her again. That was it. She was cut off. That is just terrible. I guess that was some thirty years ago. Some wounds sure do run deep, and are still waiting for time to heal them. Otis leans up to lick me. "Thanks, fella, but I'm ok."

Emme

9
SUKKOT - FEAST OF TABERNACLES

"*Prima le radici , poi le ali. First roots, then wings*" — *Italian Saying.*

A perfect day to buy some pumpkins from the little old Methodist church in town, which covers its front lawn with them for sale every October.

Emme and I are sitting on the stone steps of a small church in the historic part of town waiting for Tim and Zan and watching people. Horse drawn carriages periodically clip-clop down the street, their drivers pointing out St Augustine facts to their tourist passengers. Scruffy students from the college two blocks away ride by on their skateboards, weaving along by leaning back and forth. Across the street I can see locals heading into the barber shop that even has one of those old time striped poles outside. The sky is bright blue, the clouds are defined white puffs like in a child's drawing and the temperature is an easy 70 degrees. We've come here to buy a few pumpkins before heading to Home Depot for some 2x4's for our *sukkah* (the hut you build during the feast of tabernacles), the drugstore to pick up a prescription (allergies happen in paradise too), Target because Zan has put holes all his socks and jeans (again) and then, finally, the library. It's a family day of running errands but we seem to have stalled at our first stop.

Tim and Zander are performing some sort of male ritual of finding the perfect pumpkin that seems to take on the importance of bringing down the last bison to feed the clan. "Guys, just pick one already," I yell over to them. They are debating the merits of a few selections and barely glance up toward me. Em pipes up, "Daaad, come on. I wannnna gooo." I wish we could go to a field somewhere to pick our own, but that's not really a Florida thing. Pumpkins must be imported, and you buy them while wearing a tee shirt. There are certain sacrifices you make to live here. On the plus side, the air is never so cold that it hurts to smile and expose my teeth.

As the waiting continues I fish a pen and paper out of my purse and work on my party plans for *Sukkot*, which is pronounced *sue-COAT*, by the way. This latest and final holiday of the Jewish fall feasts comes just five days after *Yom Kippur* and it ends what is known as the *Days of Awe*. You remember that, right? When I magnanimously chose to forgive someone who really hurt me and symbolically hurled a boulder into the churning ocean, the stormy skies then cleared and rays of beatific sunlight shone upon my enlightened form? Don't bother flipping back to it. Trust me, it happened just like that.

So, here we now are: *Sukkot*, the Feast of Tabernacles and time to rejoice. We celebrate all that God has given us — food, friends, forgiveness and a roof over our heads. I happen to think this is a pretty neat spiritual journey, this trio of autumnal celebrations. There is a time set apart for examination, for sacrifice and repentance, and finally there is redemption and restoration.

I remember going to a few *Sukkah*[45] parties when I was young in our Messianic Judaism days. We went from *Sukkah* to *Sukkah* in our neighborhood, singing and eating at each one.

---

45 *Hebrew: tabernacle, singular*

JEW IN THE PEW

Traditionally, you invite friends and neighbors to join you in your *Sukkah*, even if they aren't Jewish, which is exactly what I decided to do. The other day I went to talk to Tim to tell him about my idea. I found him in the garage putting away tools that our busy son had taken out and left around. Zander had probably been building some unsanctioned project like he did last week when he had a friend sleep over. At bedtime I poked my head in his room to say goodnight. Zan was laying down reading a book. "Oh, that's nice, you're reading *(Note my tone of relief here)*. Okay, honey, goodnight," and I closed the door. My hand hadn't even left the doorknob before I realized something was wrong.

Opening the door again I said "Zander, where is Caleb?" He just pointed to the upper corner of his room. Out of a hammock hanging from hooks he had somehow screwed into the ceiling I heard, "Hi Mrs. Chandler!" I just sighed, looked at the bits of drywall on the floor, told them goodnight. All that to say that Tim routinely has to search for his tools after Zander gets a new idea. But there I was with my own new idea. "Hey Tim, what do you think about having a *Sukkot* party and making a *sukkah*, which you will have to build, of course?" "Sure. What's a sukkah?" came a calm answer amid a waist high pile of tools, gardening equipment, bikes and various garage crap.

Happy to have such an agreeable husband, I brush off a spot to sit and explained it to him while he was cleaning up. (Thank God, too, cause that place was a mess!) "Remember in the Bible when God told Moses about the Feast of Tabernacles? Well, that's what this is. Picture a box-like structure with one open side. The roof consists of gathered branches laid on top of the, spaced loosely enough that you can still see the stars. Traditionally, it is hung with fruits. This *Sukkah*, or booth, represents how God provided for our every need in our time in the wilderness and, now, during the harvest season. You know, autumn bounty and all that." He still seemed to listening, though by this point he was up on a ladder putting things back in far off spaces close to the camping equipment that's never used. I went on, "It's a seven day holiday and it's traditional to eat and sleep in the *Sukkah*." Tim stops what he's doing and looks at me skeptically, "*You* actually want to sleep outside?" "Don't be ridiculous. I'm just telling you what other people do." There is no way I am leaving my four-poster bed with the nine feather pillows for the wilds of my back yard. I stand with my father on this one; his idea of camping is having drinks by the pool.

I go on, "We'll have dinners there and I want to have a party too. The whole point is that hanging out in our little tabernacle is supposed to remind us of the precarious nature of life and how God provides." Tim agrees and tells me to draw him a diagram of what a *sukkah* is supposed to look like and he will make it. And that brings us to today's trip to Home Depot and buying pumpkins in order to build and decorate.

JEW IN THE PEW

Em is now playing a game on my cell phone. Tim has paid the nice Methodists and they're loading the car with what seems like fifty pounds of pumpkins and gourds. A new discussion springs up between Tim and Zan about where we are going to put the lumber from stop number two. I'm sitting in the front seat, staring out the window and starting to feel a little worn and with that always comes doubts that say this is a stupid idea, that I'm too late to add these Jewish observances to my kids' lives, and they won't care anyway. Taking a deep breath about the same time everyone is buckled in and we pull out of the gravel parking lot, I decide to stop listening to those worries. The truth is that those fears are slowly giving way to a bearing down feeling, a strong, internal push that's finally motivating me past decades of indecision. I've begun to take firm steps to reengage with my heritage and not just sit on the outskirts. After all, if my kids are going to have these as memories, it's up to me to create any Jewish references in their lives – no matter how daunting the enormity of it all may seem. As we drive on I feel pleased with my act of bucking myself up, cheerfully think how well the rest of today will go and start humming "Moving Right Along" from the Muppets. Zan and Tim chime in. Smiling at our happy family moment I turn around to look at the kids in the backseat. It all comes to an abrupt halt when I see Emme, who's an unfortunate nauseous car rider, is green and hear her warning. "Mom, the whole car smells of pumpkin. Uh, uh... I'm gonna be sick!" Tim slams on the breaks and at least 20 pounds of all that Autumnal bounty we just bought comes flying.

Yeah, it's all going to work out fine.

Party is tomorrow. The Chandler household is full of the sounds of building, cooking, playing and lilting background music.

I'm going to warn you right now about my mood so don't look for funny. That part of my brain is shut down right now. I'm not sad *per se*, just preoccupied and a little apprehensive. I'm in the kitchen by myself cooking for the party and listening to Pandora Radio. I don't even know what station this is. Something 1940-1960's French, mostly instrumental, little jazzy with love songs. Very sitting-in-an-outdoor-bistro-with-*un café*.

The guys are out back building. The yard is littered with lumber, power tools and a snaking bright orange extension cord. The screwdriver whines as it fastens the screw deep into the wood, there's a pause and then it sounds again as Zan hands Tim another screw, another board. Em is out front practicing her volleyball serve, smashing it off the side of the house. Thump, thump, BANG... thump, thump, BANG. I'm sure the two boys from across the street will soon appear in the driveway trying to find ways to get her attention, never realizing that she sees them as gnats to brush away. Ah, the privileged behavior of a beautiful, and capable girl who follows her own lead.

I'm an introvert by nature and need time to by myself, especially before a big party so I'm alone making my own noise of moving around the kitchen while working through what I think. There can be something meditative about cooking. It's so sensory — seeing the colors of vegetables and the changes that signify when things are cooked enough; the heavenly smell of baked goods or onions sautéed in butter; the sound of things boiling away on the stove or filling a pot with water; the feel of soft cheese or crusty bread or ripe fruit. Not when cooking is harried but at these times when I'm by myself and the rhythm of it all comes together, I let one part of my brain focus on working while another area floats somewhere else sorting troubling thoughts out.

We are beginning to make changes - which is great— but I still find myself in an emotionally odd place. On one hand, I am doing this for us, because it's part of my previously neglected heritage that I long to celebrate and be part of a Jewish community again. Plus it just kills me that I've been so remiss in exposing my children to these things. These feelings make me want to move away from all things Christian, which I find myself doing. But on the other hand, I've spent a lot of time lately in conversations with my Christian

SUKKOT - FEAST OF TABERNACLES

friends about it all because I want them to understand the great spiritual connection with God for them in these observances and feasts[46]. (Which, by the way, are never even referred to as "Jewish" feasts in the Bible but as God's feasts. Just saying.) You can see how it's sort of a push-me-pull-me. Hence, I rinse, chop, dice, sauté, bake and arrange on platters, while my mind sifts and sorts these opposing emotional ingredients. And the music plays on. As does the building and the banging.

I know that most Christians have no idea what *Sukkot* is and good chance they've never thought about Jesus celebrating it. I picture Yeshua at the Feasts, which must have been dear to Him. Possibly like parents' happiness at watching their kids enjoy a specially planned day for them. Imagine Jesus eating, singing and laughing with family and friends under a lacy canopy of palm fronds. The Messiah there, celebrating a time that is set apart to for us to acknowledge God's provision for us? Come on, seriously, that's heavy stuff. There must have been a smile across His lips. It's all so pregnant with expectancy and enjoyment and that feeling when a long awaited moment in time has finally come. I find myself smiling just thinking about it.

That is until I realize I've *almost* burnt the things in the oven. Back to focusing on the food at little more.

---

46 *See Extras at end of book.*

JEW IN THE PEW

It is traditional on *Sukkot* to eat wrapped or stuffed food because it's symbolic of fullness and bounty. For the party I've decided to make foods from around the Jewish world: Moroccan pastillo (ground chicken, eggs, nuts and spices wrapped in a phyllo dough shell), Middle-Eastern berekahs (a warm and tangy cheese pastry shaped into a triangle), spanakopita (a layered Greek dish filled with feta cheese, spinach and diced onions), knishes (round, Eastern-European street-food, filled with various, tasty morsels things depending on what country they are from — liver, onion, kasha, potato or cabbage), pita with humus, baklava (nut, honey and tissue-thin pastry dessert; popular from Turkey to North Africa), and macaroons (a flourless coconut and almond cookie said to be embraced by Italian Jews as a Passover dessert in the 1500's).

Just about the time I pull the last try out of the oven I notice that the sounds both out front and out back have abated. Time to go check on how the frame for the *Sukkah* is coming and get Em to help me start decorating. The Jewishness that I want to instill in my kids is our history, celebrations and food traditions. Without all that, life is just business and it doesn't ground us to who we are and where we come from. The world that we create in our homes today is the springboard from which children jump to their future. I don't want them to grow up and feel like they haven't been given a shot at understanding their tribe. Em suddenly comes in the door, and grabs a drink. I wash my hands, turn off the music and we both head out back to look at our newly made *Sukkah*.

Just got done cleaning up after the party. Tim and I are collapsed on the sofa. As is Otis, who spent the day sneaking food off plates.

We had a wonderful party. The family was there, of course, and then about 15 - 20 friends from church. The *Sukkah* looked beautiful in our backyard garden. The roof was made with bamboo and palm fronds laid across the top. Decorative apples, pears and grapes dangled above our heads from ribbons tied to the roof, as the side curtains billowed in the ocean breeze. Since we had so many people who could not all sit inside, I put a buffet in there. A long folding table was covered with burlap all the way to the grass but on top I made shelves of various levels for different platters of food. All that was draped with a cranberry colored cloth while smaller pumpkins and mums and sunflowers tucked into little spots. It definitely had the look of Fall bounty. I made little signs to place at seating areas to help our friends understand about *Sukkot*, its symbolism, history and relevance. Everyone seemed to have a good time. The happy sounds of talking and laughing filled the back yard, billowing over the flowerbeds and then up our tall white fences and into the air.

I was touched that many of our Christian friends mentioned they felt honored to be invited. Their total unfamiliarity of *Sukkot* has rung a somewhat minor chord to an otherwise cheerful melody for two reasons. It just shouldn't be this way. They should be taught about this within the church, same as they teach their congregations about other God-stuff. And I wish I could share this festival with other Jews besides my family. Maybe this time next year things will be a little different and I won't be in a position of having to introduce the holiday, but we will celebrate within a community who already knows. But these are the people I see most weekends, have been in Bible studies with, and have known for years. They are dear friends, the spiritual community in which God has now placed me. It made sense that we should all be together to celebrate a beautiful holiday that God created.

At some point during the day, I noticed one of the platters was getting low and went to refill it. Ellen saw and followed me into the kitchen. "I can't believe you went to all this trouble," she says in between bites of baklava, which she had just lifted off the tray I was arranging neatly. "I mean it's lovely and all that. So, uh, you're really getting into the Jewish stuff here, aren'tcha?" I tried to explain about my decision to do Jewish things this year and finally dealing with this issue, all the while grabbing things out of the fridge and various cabinets – extra napkins, more food, toothpicks, etc. But she wasn't really listening. She started telling a story that had absolutely nothing to do with what I just said and then wandered back outside to join the party. I looked down at Otis as if to say, "What was *that* about?" But then I realized his attention on me was less about solidarity then it was about the baklava tray I was working on. "Forget it, Otis. Don't think I didn't see all the food you've been eating." His tail and ears drooped as he followed me back outside to the party.

Tim and Otis are both now snoring away. The kids have flittered off. Emme is upstairs in her room and Zan went to the beach with some buddies to skim board before it gets dark. I just finished quietly wandering around picking up stray plastic cups, wrapping up the leftovers and evaluating the day. I thought about something my friend Allison said. She goes to our church and is also Jewish and married a Gentile, but is not practicing any Judaism in her life at all. She said she was misty-eyed because she hasn't been in a *Sukkah* since her childhood and it felt profound to be here, but also sad, as these things aren't part of her life. My heart has often had that very same ache. It's like a dense dusky purple cloud and only at its edges can you see through it. I think it's the pervading sorrow of loss of something meaningful, warm and treasured. Previously, I have always felt powerless against that melancholy purple haze, because past circumstances and choices made for me or by me, had lopped off my options. Or so I thought.

But now my actions of late have shown me that doing something, although difficult and not ideal, is far better than doing nothing and letting the cloud settle in. We built the *Sukkah* to celebrate God's gifts to us, to follow the commandment, to reconnect, and to show on the outside that I am as Jewish as I feel on the inside. From my sofa vantage point, I look through the open French doors to the back yard where the *Sukkah* stands. The curtain sides are still swaying with the breeze, the bamboo on top hangs down a bit in the front looking like untrimmed bangs. All is quiet now, cleaned up and pleasant. In wafts a sense of a job well done. I lean up against Tim, who instinctively puts his arm around me though he's still asleep. The peace and spiritual renewal I feel is an unexpected gift and there's not a cloud in the sky. Seems like a perfect time to rest and take a nap.

It feels like an autumn day. Cool, breezy, even the sunlight looks different. It isn't that full head-on brightness, but the slanted golden kind of sunshine.

I open the window over my desk and look out while I wait for my computer to turn on. Somehow, it seems like there is a change of season in the air even though the trees, grass, everything all look the same. Suddenly a ping notifies me I have email to read. Nothing from Rick. I had sent my brother a beautiful family picture of Tim and me and the kids in our *Sukkah*. I wonder what he thought. Periodically, he shoots out some pretty acerbic barbs ridiculing me for incorporating Jewish things, when I clearly live a mostly Christian life. I realize he's angry and bitter that Mom left synagogue when he was a teenager, but his actions increase the alienation. Sometimes I think he has the view that if he shows us enough venom for our way of life we will wake up and stop all the interfaith intertwining and be who *he* thinks we should be.

A breeze blows a few papers around. I stop their departure by rearranging a couple of silver picture frames on top of them — the yellowed picture of Rick kissing my chubby check when he was eight and I was two, the happy snapshot of Tim and me on a trip to Italy some years back, and a small one of Zander and Tim's dad heading off for a walk in the woods together, two buddies born 60 years apart. I pull up our *Sukkot* picture on my computer. We all look happy. Maybe I'll frame this one too. Here's another one with just the girls — Gra, Mom, El, and me and our daughters. That's four generations of believing Jews under the *Sukkah*.

Another breeze flutters the now pinned down papers. I glance at Rick's picture again and sigh. We all enjoyed Sukkot so much, why can't Rick be happy for us instead of irritated? I'm sure it would be easier for him if we never did anything Jewish or never did anything Christian but the fact that we do both is just heresy because, according to him, you can't be both. Well, I want to be both. We are both. And with that thought, I make the picture of all us girls my desktop photo.

Lunch time. Just got home. Really in the mood for a nice Corned-Beef Special. No luck. Have to settle for a ham and cheese sandwich. How symbolic.

I couldn't wait to get home from Bible study to write out my thoughts. But now that I am home, all I feel like doing is *not* thinking. That's the danger of not being able to process stirred up thoughts right away. They have a limited shelf life in terms of accessibility. What may be keys to clearing emotional murkiness can quickly return to brain sludge. Knowing this, I am going to force myself to tell you about my morning while I make myself some lunch.

I went to Bible study at church this morning. Which was fine. Except it wasn't. I went thinking our *Sukkot* success would buffet me against the usual church chaffing. But, maybe it made it worse. It actually started last night during a very honest tête-à-tête between God and myself. Although, let's be honest, I was the one who did most of the talking.

I told Him that I want to pursue this Jewish thing, but it mucks up how I feel about Him. I've started to wonder (i.e. worry, because that's my default setting) what this will cost my current relationship with God. I asked us both, "Do I view You as Jewish or Christian?"

I feel this separation because there is just so much history that gets left out in church life — what gets preached, and in conversations and interactions with Christians — so it almost seems that we are talking about two different deities. The Christian one is mostly that three-quarters-of-an-inch, New Testament part at the back of the Bible, whose worship songs seem mostly to pray to only Jesus. (Didn't He himself say we should pray to God and not to him[47]?) The Christian God just seems so modern, so GOD 7.0 — as if it's an upgrade from the original version that generated all those system errors. Somewhere along the line Yeshua the Jew magically became Jesus the uber-polite, Protestant with blue eyes and impossibly good posture. I don't even like that picture. It's so small, so un-God. Well, except for the good posture but not in that spinal fusion stiff sort of way, you know?

Speaking of being upright, if I don't eat something soon I'm going fall right over. The sound of the pantry opening brings Otis running. "No, it's not for you. This is *my* lunch." Wagging with a deep look of hope in his puppy dog brown eyes seals it. "Ok, fine. You

---

47 *Matthew 6:6-9*

want a treat?" What a stupid question. No chewies to be found so the lucky little guy gets some old cheese I find rummaging in the fridge. I really need to go food shopping. And where did this lunchmeat come from?

Where was I? Oh, right, God. I recognize that as a Jewish believer in Yeshua I really have both halves here, which is great. But it doesn't feel like it when sitting in church. In church, I pray in Jesus' name and all that, but I tend to be picturing that Sunday school, meek Anglo God. When it's Shabbat, a Jewish holiday, or when I am at home, it's different. Then He's the God of Abraham, Isaac and Jacob. This is the God who's got a little *shtick*,[48] who expects a Jew to argue with Him and is very big picture — beginning to end. So, to me, God is the whole thing, not just the last half of the Bible. It has to go together. It's like He has laid out the most amazing dramatic show though we, in the present time, have only just sat down in the second act. Here's the whole theater analogy. At church it feels everyone watching is sure they just don't need to know what happened before they (Christians) showed up on the scene. But who wants to come to a play and miss the first half? What kind of story is it if all the character development and story nuances from the first act are disposable? But there I am, well aware of what happened before Intermission. "Oh man, this is so great! Remember the foreshadowing when

---

48 *Yiddish: humor, personality, character*

SUKKOT - FEAST OF TABERNACLES

God…" And then I get the wave of the hand to knock it off and calm down, "Shhhh. We don't need to know that. " Eager to tie it all together, I try again, "No, really, it's good stuff…" I'm cut off. "Be quiet now. It's only the now that matters."

In Bible study this morning, Beth Moore spoke about Jacob wrestling with the angel. I could relate. That is how I feel about this whole issue. Struggling, struggling, wrestling and I just will not let go until God blesses me. Ya know, maybe it's not coincidental that my hip has been hurting … *hmm* …

Curled up on my swivel rocker, laptop perched on my knees. It's a grey morning. The ocean sounds rough. Must go for a beach walk later and see if something interesting has churned up.

The ride to take the kids to school this morning was just a continuation of what kind of mood everyone was in last night. Must be the weather. Let me tell you, I couldn't get to that drop off line fast enough. It was delicious moment when they gathered up book bags, and lunches and things and shut the car door behind them, leaving me in silence on the inside. The route home along Coastal Highway was uneventful, except for the predictable road crossings for this kind of day. When storms come you drive down A1A dodging surfers running to the beach like otters ready to jump down the slide into the pond at the zoo.

I'm ready to start working on a new writing piece — Otis by my side snoring and laptop in front of me – but I'm mulling over yesterday. It was *Simchat Torah*, the holiday[49] that celebrates the Torah, and finishes and begins the reading cycle in synagogue. During the service the Torah is taken out, and paraded around with singing, dancing and flags waving. It's a very joyous service. Earlier in the day I toyed with the idea of going to synagogue after dinner but that's certainly not how the evening went.

It was a rainy and windy night. For dinner I made beef soup with barley and baby Portobello mushrooms that we ate with crusty baguette slices. At the table, I tried to ask Tim about his day but was interrupted by Zander sharing every thought in his head. Then Emme felt the need to interject by telling him how stupid and immature he was. Otis was barking to be let out with all the urgency of a hunting dog. A fat bullfrog had made the really bad decision to hop into the light of the back door. It all was getting a bit tedious. Rain and frog be damned, I got up to let the dog out and see if we had any Pinot Noir left. The kids, meanwhile, continued to provoke one another as only siblings can do. As I brought back some wine for Tim and me, I

---

[49] *Simchat Torah is not a Biblical holy day. It was added later.*

SUKKOT - FEAST OF TABERNACLES

mentioned the *Simchat Torah* service that was to start in an hour. No one was interested *at all*. I instantly dropped the idea in favor of going to bed early with a good book on such a dark and damp night.

This morning I realize that I'm relieved we didn't go. Last time I was there, on *Yom Kippur*, I enjoyed it so much — the Jewish faces, the prayers, seeing the men wearing their *tallises*[50], and being in a building where Jews have been worshiping God for a hundred years — that I fear I might enjoy it *even more* and feel even more pulled in two directions. But that's confusing because really they aren't two different directions. It's one God. It's just that tricky Messiah bit. Most Jews are still waiting for the Messiah, but I'm not. I've got that part taken care of. This really makes a point for the idea of Messianic Judaism. It seems there must be a place for Jewish believers to go, and not have to give up living like a Jew; somewhere that we don't have to translate our culture, our history, High Holy Days, our worship or downplay the *Tanach*.

I feel alone and between worlds, like the surfers running across the highway. Except they are a pretty carefree bunch who carry their own floatation devices and catch up with likeminded people once in the water. So, I guess the parallel doesn't really work. Although, I do have inner tubes in the garage. Not the same thing though.

---

50 *Hebrew: prayer shawls*

"Two sisters" Ellen and Jenny

10
FRIDAY NIGHT DINNERS

"MORE THAN THE JEWS HAVE KEPT SHABBAT, SHABBAT
HAS KEPT THE JEWS."
— AHAD HA'AM.

Friday night. The stars are shining brightly. It was cool, very quiet and lovely out.

Even though I just took a 15-minute walk in my neighborhood, dog in tow, I didn't see any of it.

JEW IN THE PEW

Not the driveways I passed, not the bush Otis stopped at, not even the kids' bikes left out. As soon I left our warm and bright kitchen and stepped into the cool night, I was lost in reverie. Maybe it was the way the air felt outside tonight or how the stars looked but something reminded me of *Shabbat (Sabbath)* dinners at my grandmother's house when I was young. As I walked along with the leash in one hand a cup of hot chocolate in the other I went back in time.

Every Friday after school I would drop my things off at home and then immediately head next door. I was down our two front steps and over to my grandparents' front door by the time our screen would slam shut behind me. Late afternoon light streamed in their lace curtains and all would be neat and clean except where my grandfather was sitting. He would be in the living room playing the cello or the piano, music sheets piled high or sitting on the sofa surrounded by books, magazines and papers. "Hi Pop-Pop," I would say as I bent down to kiss his upturned check. This had to be done carefully. A pencil was often behind his ear hidden by his unruly hair. I have no idea what notes he was forever taking.

I then made a beeline for the kitchen to see Gra getting ready for *Shabbat*. She would be listening to "Friday with Frank," a weekly radio show that ran for 40 years in the Philadelphia area where we then lived, as she rubbed butter on a chicken ready to go in the oven. *Shabbat* to me means Sinatra in the background, a clean house, and the smell of a nice roasted chicken. Gra thought Frank was quite something; I think she had a big crush on him for like 40 or 50 years. Besides, he was Italian, which is just like being Jewish but with less persecution. They have that same special *patois* of food, guilt and family opinions. By the time night fell, we all would be around their table, lighting the candles, eating and talking all at once.

It was always the same routine after Shabbat dinner. Pop-pop and Uncle Michael went into the living room to talk. Ellen and I (Rick had moved out of the house by then) would clear the dishes from the table, often while singing. Gra rinsed the dishes in the sink under a window framed by yellow curtains with purple violets growing on the sill. Mom put away the leftovers — chicken in Tupperware, extra *challah* back in the bag from Greenberg's, butter back in the fridge — all while going on and on about something or another to her mom. (Maybe that's where Zan gets it from?).

It was my job to take the tablecloth outside to shake out the crumbs. It was always too warm inside my grandmother's house. I'd like to think that it was the glow of the *Shabbat* candles, our singing, or the steamy chicken. But really it was because my grandfather was forever on blood thinners that made him sensitive to cold. And so, the house was kept much too hot for everyone else. The fact that Pop-Pop *could* have put on a sweater was not even an option. No, instead we all had to suffer.

JEW IN THE PEW

When I opened the front door to shake out the tablecloth, the night air cooled my hot checks. Looking up into the sky, I'd always think about how I was cleaning up after *Shabbat* just like other little Jewish girls all around the world, and for thousands of years before me. Although I was young, my sense of being connected was both profound and treasured. There was never a question of what you were doing on Friday night. We were doing what we always did — having dinner as a family, and then going to Shabbat services just like everyone else we knew.

Truthfully, even though I felt a great sense of belonging, there were many times I was a little bored, especially if for some reason Stacy wasn't at services. Then I'd have to find another friend to sit with but she was the best for writing notes and giggling, while adults turned around and told us to *shhh*. That, of course, made us laugh even more. The thing that makes my smile suddenly fade after thinking about these times, is that my kids don't have any of those fond *Shabbat* memories. In all our busyness and rush in life and, of course, with the church going, I realize that I never stopped and created even a bit of all that I had for Emme and Zander.

Coming back in the door, I take off Otis' leash and hang it up. He walks into the living room while wagging looking like he's telling everyone what a nice time we had. I follow a few seconds behind him, not exactly in the same mood. He had wandered down the street but I had wandered down memory lane and then suddenly realized I've neglected to lead my kids down a certain well-worn Jewish path.

Another week gone by. Tomorrow is Shabbat. Or should I say today as now it's 1:00 AM.

Since that fateful walk back to Gra and Pop-pop's table of yesteryear, I've been thinking about *Shabbat* a lot. I decided to bring this all up to Tim as we were getting ready for bed when he has a big meeting tomorrow. Of course, I didn't remember that until later. Still, this is progress because most of the time I wait until he is almost fully asleep when I turn to him and say, "Tim? You awake? I've been thinking."

The kids were asleep and Otis was on our bed as we came into the bedroom and closed the door behind us. Tim went into his walk-in closet to change and I called out, "Hey, um, so I decided I'd like to have *Shabbat* be more of a thing in our lives." Now, I'm off to my closet to change. Tim comes out in his boxers and a t-shirt. "What do you mean?" and begins to wash his face. Otis watches us back and forth from his spot on Tim's pillow. I come out a minute later in my cute little pajama bottoms and a cami. Tim turns around and gives me a look that tells me he would really rather do something else than have this conversation. But like wives throughout time who have something they want to talk about when their husbands have another idea, I keep talking and swat his hands away. "Tim, I'm trying to talk about something." He sighs, grabs the floss and says, "We go to church on Sunday. Can't that be our Sabbath?" While washing my face I take a minute to compose my words because that response kind of ticked me off a little. It was just so gentile-Christianity-centered.

Patting my face dry, I start to explain while reaching for the first of my many various creams that all claim to miraculously stave off aging of one kind or another. "For the first couple of hundred years the gathering of the believers was always on *Shabbat*, after all they were predominately Jews. It wasn't until the fourth century when the Gentile followers of Jesus vastly outnumbered those who were Jewish that 'the Church' declared Sunday to be a day of worship instead of Saturday." Tim has been brushing his teeth and I take his silence as an invitation to continue versus merely an act of oral hygiene. "Ya know, quite a bit of anti-Semitism came into play there. They (Bishops gathered at the council of Nicea) actually told Christians to *not* be like the Jews but to work on Saturday. And the clergy were even forbidden conversation or fellowship with a Jew! From then on the gathering of believers and partaking of the Lord's Table was moved to Sunday." I'm riled up just talking about the decisions made by these long dead guys. "Nice one, there boys, I'm sure that made the God of the Jews very pleased. Oh, I'm sorry, was that the very same God you were trying to worship?" As soon as I said that I knew I shouldn't have. Tim looked weary and clearly given up hope of derailing my state of mind to marital playfulness. He might as well join the conversation.

"Jenny, don't you think it's it important that we follow the spirit of the law about worshipping together and not the letter of the law?" I answer him while pulling out the floss. "Yeah, yeah, I get that it's more important *who* we worship and not *when* we worship. But you have to understand that these kinds of things — these deliberate "The Parting of the Ways[51]" have caused a lot of damage. Would the Crusades and Inquisition have happened if Constantine and the other Christian big wigs *not* decreed that all church practices should be moved away from Judaism?" My blue fingertips alert me that in my diatribe I absentmindedly over-wrapped the floss. Tim is trying to find where I'm going with all this: "So, now you want to change when church has their day of worship?" I answer, "No, that's ridiculous. They don't have to become Jews. What I am trying to express is how it feels when Christians ask me why I can't just have my Sabbath on Sunday like the rest of the church. It's like someone took something that was rightfully mine, sold it to strangers, and is now asking me to buy it back."

---

51 *That was the official term for separating the Church from it's Jewish origins during the Council of Nicea.*

JEW IN THE PEW

By this point we are standing at either side of the bed. Just like every other night, Tim picks up Otis who is giving him sad puppy dog eyes that beg to be left right where he is. Instead, he is put on the floor. Turning down the sheets I point out that Sunday does not feel restful to me. Sundays mean getting up early, getting everyone dressed and out the door on time, coming home after church, finishing up some things around the house. He mows the lawn or washes the car. I've got to straighten up the house so we don't start the week in disarray, making sure the kids are ready for school tomorrow, homework is finished, uniforms are clean, carpool planned, etc. Doing all that does not make me feel that I have set aside a special time as God commanded, to honor Him, appreciate our family, and have a *Shabbat*. Tim tells me he's done with the conversation and has an early day tomorrow. We kiss goodnight, roll away from each other to turn off our bedside table lamps and Otis lets out a sigh. Tim instantly falls asleep. I lay there in the dark…thinking.

Reason #8 Why I Love St Augustine: Pirates next to you in line at the library.

The coffee table is now covered with books from the library. Cookbooks mostly. My reading topics go in spurts. There was the summer I read all about cheeses.

FRIDAY NIGHT DINNERS

A couple months ago I was plowing through books on neuroscience and moods. There was the Kennedy White House phase, the memoirs of ex-pats living in Italy or France period, and, of course, the ongoing Jewish learning which pretty much takes up a good percentage of my bookshelves. I know, I'm just the kind of person you want to invite to your next party, right? Nothing says fun like the woman who after a drink or two starts talking about how impressed she is with some guy's brain after reading his latest sociology book.

This afternoon I went to our local library to pick up five or six books on my latest interest: baking bread (specifically *Challah*[52]) and traditional Jewish recipes. Because St Augustine is a historical tourist town there tend to be lots of characters around. This means on any given day you could be in the bank next to man in a British militia uniform outdated by maybe 200 years. Or, say, like today, as I was standing in front of the New Releases, the lady reaching for the romance novel to my right was dressed in a laced up bodice, skirt to the floor with a pewter mug dangling from her waist. I felt a little underdressed next to her in my jeans and tank top. Besides I never bring my tankard with me on errands.

The Friday night after our little bedtime talk didn't go so well. Here's what I wanted: a lovely

---

52 *Traditional braided egg bread served on Shabbat.*

JEW IN THE PEW

Shabbat dinner with a white tablecloth, using the nice dishes, a big meal, a clean house and an interested interactive family. Here's what actually happened. The end of the week snuck up on us. The kid's backpacks and a week's worth of papers were strewn everywhere, Otis barking at the doorbell when the pizza delivery guy came while some insipid TV show was blaring from the living room and absolutely no one paying any attention to the fact that I was trying to say the blessing over the candles and wedge in a little ceremony. Needless to say that week the whole Shabbat thing felt pretty forced and devoid of any importance. To top it all off they got our order wrong and dropped off a pizza with sausage and pineapple. Ughh.

I wound up sitting alone in the kitchen with a picked apart piece of pizza by the light of the Shabbat candlesticks that my great-grandmother brought with her from Russia. It was time to do some more reevaluating. Or at least better planning. Hence, the cookbooks. I've decided as a step to the Shabbat evenings that I want to happen around here I'm going to master making *Challah*. Although I have tried numerous times I have yet to get it down. I'm not even sure what the problem is there. How hard can it be to make bread? I bet that lady in the Colonial outfit in the library can do it. I should have asked her for some tips.

FRIDAY NIGHT DINNERS

Yet another Friday. Haircut today at 9 AM. Dinner at friends at 6 PM.

I had time before my appointment and spent it walking around St Augustine, taking in the fresh morning air and quiet streets. Few people were about — a jogger puffing by, a *sous* chef on the way to work, a woman sweeping off a step. Without the crowds, I could more appreciate the worn blue shutters and the fuchsia bougainvillea climbing a wall, scattering its petals like confetti on the ground below. It was too early for the horse-drawn carriages that clip clop down the cobbled stone streets. The only sounds I heard were my own footsteps, as I walked past pots of flowers still blooming this warm November day. Feeling relaxed and peaceful I thought that in moments like this when the sky is so blue and I am breathing deeply that my whole Jewish/Christian dilemma isn't so important.

That was until I got a phone call from my brother. While chatting away I stupidly mentioned something about our botched Shabbat last week. Before I knew it, Rick was lambasting me for how I am raising my children. Damn, and I was having such a nice day. Even my hair looks great. I finally hung up and called Ellen to vent. "What is his problem? He doesn't say these things to you!" Now, keep in mind that although

JEW IN THE PEW

Ellen and I both believe in Yeshua, she is far more comfortable in the Christian world. She doesn't miss Jewish stuff as much as I. Not because she doesn't think it is important but mostly because not much really bothers her. Ever. Well, that's not exactly true. She feels really strongly that responsible people should always choose wheat bread. And recycling. She's very committed to recycling. But besides that there just aren't many views she can't see the other side of. You remember, of course, that she is the middle child. "I don't know, Jenn. I guess Rick just can't stand that you do both Jewish stuff *and* Christian stuff." Ughh, so frustrating. Some sibling solidarity would have felt nice. Then again, she doesn't understand why I need to organize my spice cabinet, either. Well, this still doesn't deter me from bringing more Shabbat in our lives.

Tonight we are invited to have dinner at the house of one of our church friends. Even though I love to be in their company it's Friday and they aren't Jewish. So, sadly, this means no Shabbat for us. Apparently I was not really facing that fact half an hour ago when I put a tiny, frozen unbaked (i.e. raw dough) *Challah* in the oven on low to defrost it and have it rise. The package said to bake it after 4-6 hours. What was I thinking? There isn't enough time to get this done properly. Should I take our little *Challah*-in-a-box to dinner tonight? If I had made it myself that would have been okay. Not that I would have boxed it had I made it myself. But to plunk down a diminutive partially revived, cryogenic loaf whose symbolism would mean nothing to them is just plain odd. That's just not a proper hostess gift. Note to self: Buy flowers.

Maybe the bread will be done in time for us to say a *Barucha*[53] and leave it at home before we go. I'm frustrated on so many levels right now. Even my hair has started to droop. Staring at that sad excuse for bread through the little oven window I feel like Scarlett O'Hara: "As God as my witness I will make my own *Challah* one day!" The music starts. The camera pulls back to the silhouette of me standing alone on a hill, the shriveled-up, frozen lump of dough in my hand raised to the sky. Fade to black. Queue the music.

---

53 *Hebrew: blessing*

My nephew Jordan with Zander

11
WRESTLING

Rabbi Zusha used to say: "When I die and come before the heavenly court, if they ask me, 'Zusha, why were you not Abraham?' I'll say that I didn't have Abraham's intellectual abilities. If they say, 'Why were you not Moses?' I'll say I didn't have Moses' leadership abilities. For every such question, I'll have an answer. But if they say, 'Zusha, why were you not Zusha?' for that, I'll have no answer."

JEW IN THE PEW

Monday. 9:30 pm. Writing in bed. Kids are asleep. Tim is downstairs finishing up some work. Otis is snoring next to me.

Tonight Zander was watching the History Channel when a show about the Crusaders came on. Like me, he loves history, and what boy doesn't like knights. But I asked him to change the channel. I wasn't in the mood to watch a show about European "Christians" waging a bloody war against Jews and Muslims in an effort to take back Jerusalem from the "infidels". He was confused. "Why? Mom, knights and armor are cool, and attacking bad guys is cool." I asked him to just mute it a sec so I could explain. "Zan, in real life the Crusades were a terrible bloodbath. Even though it was just supposed to be fought in the Holy Land, it actually triggered a great deal of persecution of Jews all over Europe. Horrible things were done while calling Jews Christ killers."

Zander yelled, a little out of passion but also because the kid is just plain loud, "That is *sooo* stupid! Didn't they read their Bibles? The Romans killed Jesus." I reminded him that it was Jews who told Pilate to crucify him. The rabid cry for the inhumane murder of man who did no wrong is truly a low point in our history. Well, Zan didn't think that made all Jews responsible – which is true, of course. I could tell that he was finding the idea of Jews being abused by knights confusing. After all, there are knight play sets and books about these guys, and besides they were Christians, right? He looked confused and upset.

Staring down at my son, watching him grapple with this new information I wondered how he was identifying himself at that moment. Was he thinking of himself more as the Christian on horseback or as the persecuted Jew? Finally, all Zan could say was that it just didn't make sense. I gave him the only answer I have about genocide — whether it's the 1100's or the 1940's. "Evil doesn't make sense, honey. And there is no way to figure it out no matter how hard you try, because evil is evil." We changed the channel to watch an old episode of *Myth Busters*. The tension left the room as we watched them destroy something, this time in the name of science.

Ironically, and somewhat thematically, the word "crusade" came up in church yesterday, as one of the pastors shared about a mission trip. I winced. Was I the only one in the room who did? I honestly cannot fathom why any Christian, even Billy Graham, would ever use that word. You'd think that an ordained minister would have been educated in the full history of the Church and not just the pleasant parts. Of course, I realize the word "crusade" can be used as in campaign, fight or movement; but it seems to me a poor choice of words. It's quite alienating to any Jew or Arab within earshot because these people know full well of the horrible atrocities committed in the name of Christ. Education in Christian persecution tends to be all one-sided – from Nero, on down to today's

JEW IN THE PEW

Chinese believers. This is important, but shouldn't the truth *also* be taught that for thousands of years the Church persecuted God's Chosen People? For the Jew sitting in a church, there is this very apparent disconnect. We are painful aware of history that our pew-buddy to the right and left of us are not. But I doubt many mainstream-comfortable Christians ever think about that. This is a sad thing to write about before bedtime. I think I will go read Psalms before I fall asleep. That will make me feel better.

Upper 70's right now. Shorts and t-shirt weather. Theses are the days for which we live in Florida and battle through the summer heat.

It's late November and Otis and I are at the beach — bright sunshine and crashing waves. We have some time before the kids come home from school, so I came to journal my thoughts that Bible study triggered this morning. Otis is here for the smells. He sits facing the wind, ears flapping away, black button nose twitching away at all the scents coming up the coast. You got to wonder what exactly is he thinking about? As I rake the sand with my fingers I think about other sandy places. Deserts though. Egypt. Sinai.

This morning, I was struck by something Christian author Beth Moore said in her study, *The Patriarchs*.

She was speaking about Joseph's time in Pharaohs court and wrote, "After all, he dressed the part of an Egyptian on the outside, but deep inside Hebrew blood still coursed through his veins. A secret war waged within." These are my feelings exactly within the church. For all those years that I didn't want to address this nagging Jewish/Christian identity thing, it was creating a secret war within. I tried in the Episcopal Church to ignore how my Jewish thinking differed from theirs. Then I tried in the non-denominational church to ignore that they never recognized the Feasts. I even tried not going to church at all but then I missed that feeling of sharing God-stuff with people who also devoted their lives to following Him. Like I told you, I was sort of propelled out of Messianic Judaism because of events beyond my control. And, out of my pain I had looked back at Messianic Judaism as a bad idea, a conglomeration that became something less than its original two parts — Judaism and belief in Jesus. Now that it has been over 25 years and I've explored multiple streams of Christianity and Judaism, I am seeing things differently. Sure, it's not perfect or mainstream or whatever. But I can tell you this — Messianic Judaism *does* meet a need. Even though Christians are my siblings in spirit, I absolutely ache for my holidays, traditions of worship, and history without all the Anglo wash. When you are a Jew, it matters. I believe you can turn it off for a season, but it's like a genetic time bomb – at some point the switch is flipped.

JEW IN THE PEW

Even though I feel badly for Moses — Seriously, who would want Moses' job? — I'm pretty much going to blame him for this phenomenon. There's this conversation between God and Moses in Exodus 33:16-17 that explains it. They are face to face in the tabernacle and Moses has had just about enough of *schlepping*[54] these *kvetchers*[55] all over the dessert. He's tired and worried that if God doesn't put His stamp on us and set us apart from the nations of the earth we will be unprotected and disappear. Clearly, God is on board with the idea and agrees. So *poof!* It's thousands of years later, and we Jews are still set apart – no matter if we are in a church or not. Somehow, it just still matters. It's like a spiritually genetic God thing. I suppose if you want a further explanation you'll have to go ask Moses. Be assured, when I get to heaven I'm going to. He couldn't have asked for something else?

Thanksgiving Day. By 10 AM the house was bustling as we all went about getting ready.

Tim, Zan and my nephew Jordan (who slept over last night) brought in folding chairs from the garage, and then put the extension in the dining-room table.

---

54 *Yiddish: dragging*
55 *Yiddish: complainers*

This made a lot of noise — things falling over in the garage, chairs knocking against walls on their way in, scrapping on the floor of moving the table around. Meanwhile Emme and I cooked. She was in charge of making the pumpkins pies. And I was seasoning the turkey, and making Texan cranberry sauce. It's a new recipe I'm trying, with diced jalapeño and crushed pineapple. I have no idea if they actually eat this in Texas but that is what it's called. Otis was in charge of getting underfoot and licking up pumpkin splatters off the floor. In the midst of all this we wound up in a conversation about America's Founding Fathers. Emme had been learning about them in school, and Tim and I had recently watched the *John Adams* miniseries[56].

A great sacrifice was paid in order to live according to their beliefs. I silently wondered if I felt the same way about being Jewish? For thousands and thousands of years, my people have believed it was so important to be Jews and to follow God's will, that they greatly suffered for it. With enormous determination, those of previous generations fought to resist assimilation no matter where they lived. Do I pattern my life to uphold that which was so costly to those before me in a long tribal line tracing back to Abraham? To be honest, I'm afraid I haven't. And with that thought I slid the turkey into the oven.

---

56 *Great show, by the way. I still can't believe the surgery his daughter went through for breast cancer. OMG.*

JEW IN THE PEW

A few years ago, we started this tradition of going for a walk while the turkey cooks. It's a nice family activity, and, more importantly, it creates a caloric deficit prior to the gorging. After the table was set and the pies were done, Em retreated to her room for a little peace and quiet. We went to the beach so Zan and Jordan could run around before they had to sit at a table. While they were tackling each other on the shore like two young lion cubs, Tim and I went for a walk down the beach. "Don't hurt each other!" I called over my shoulder. "Ok!" they both said in unison and continued to be a blur of arms, legs, sand, laughing and grunting. We pretty much have been having that same conversation since the boys were about five years old. I'm not even sure why I still bother to say it. Sometimes I mix it up a bit and say, "I'm not taking anyone to the Emergency Room today so don't get hurt." For some reason they think that's funny.

The weather was lovely — mild and warm — just right for a beach stroll. We headed toward the water's edge, hand in hand, the sun sparkled off the ocean. I wondered if this would be a good time to tell him that in my prayers of late, would he join me in learning more about Judaism. But I was afraid that saying so would bring up our premarital discussions of so many years ago when I had assured him that the whole Jewish thing wasn't an issue and I really wanted to marry him no matter what. Since it was such a beautiful day and a holiday, I decided to give Tim a break and not bring it up.

Uncharacteristically, I quietly walked alongside him. Then, out of our amiable silence, Tim tells me that while reading his Bible that morning he felt God urging him to head toward a new territory. It suddenly seemed like the right time to share how much it would mean to me to have his involvement in my journey. (So much for keeping things to myself.) His response floored me. He said, "Okay, hand me a stack of books and I'll read them." I stopped mid-stride and hugged him, almost crying. This meant so much to me. "Thank you," was all I could whisper. What a wonderful beginning to Thanksgiving. I have a lot to be thankful for. We then turned around and walked back to the boys in the sand, and back to home to the turkey in the oven.

Black Friday. I got up this morning at 6:00 AM to go shopping. I bagged some great deals and was on my way back home by 9:00 AM.

I think Black Friday shopping definitely qualifies as a Proverbs 31 thing. After all, I did rise before dawn and bought things for my family from afar, even if 'afar' was only Target. When I came home to pajama-clad sleepy people still feeling groggy from last night's tryptophan excess. I made a mental note that they better perk up later because Tim and I agreed that tonight — it's *Shabbat* — we would visit the synagogue I went to on

JEW IN THE PEW

Yom Kippur. Just like the other week, this also didn't go according to my daydreams. The kids balked at going. Our Sabbath meal consisted of turkey leftovers warmed on the stove. Everyone came and got their own meal, while that damned TV droned on and on. I hate that stupid thing sometimes. No candles were lit; no blessing over the wine was recited. But at 7:00 p.m. we got in the car to go to services.

In the car I could feel myself stiffening up, just waiting for a comment that was going to hurt and showing me how the kids didn't care about this like I did. I tried to relax, took a deep breath and unclenched my hands. I told myself it doesn't matter that we didn't have a real *Shabbat* dinner; what matters is that we are trying. "Life is a journey, not a destination," I reminded my perfectionist self. By the way, that particular self really needs to give me a break — the older I get the more I see what a controlling killjoy that mentality is. Speaking of which, Emme was sullen and making snarky comments about going in the hope that we would just turn around. Tim gave my hand a little squeeze, and whispered, "Relax. Ignore her. It will be fine." Zan was asking question after question after question on the way. Instead of feeling glad that he was trying to learn, I felt accused. His ignorance of Jewish things could only mean it was my fault in not teaching him earlier. Surely there was a big neon sign over my head flashing "bad Jewish mother."

By the time we walked inside and sat down on those worn wooden seats I was happy to be there and could breathe normally. The people were welcoming and, again, it felt warm, soothing and peaceful in the room. I saw Lillian with her pendulous eyelashes and wondered if she remembered our conversation. To her I was probably just another visitor in the crowd; to me she was a voice of acceptance. It was the 50th wedding anniversary of a beloved couple that had long been members of the synagogue. The rabbi didn't speak, a close friend of theirs shared instead. He opened with a joke: A man sees a large watch-face hanging in a store window so he goes in to get his watch fixed. The guy behind that counter says he can't do that, because he isn't a watchmaker. The man asks, "So then, why do you have a watch in your window?" The reply, "I'm a *Mohel*.[57] What would you have me put there instead?" Everyone laughed. I like being a part of a people who could laugh at things like that, without feeling the need to be prudish. I've noticed that Christians don't joke much about penises.

The rest of the service was nice. We followed along in the *Siddur*, the prayer book, which was easier for me than for Tim since he knows absolutely no Hebrew. We sang, we read in response, stood, sat, listened and turned pages but left before it was over. I may have been ready to leave even before Tim. Although I

---

[57] *A rabbi who performs circumcisions*

loved hearing the Hebrew and seeing those genetically familiar faces, I felt only filled to a point. Like when you can't wait to eat that chocolate cake, finally take a few bites and then realize it isn't doing it for you, as you thought it would. I was glad we had gone, but after a while I was ready to go home and kick off my shoes, both physically and spiritually. Nothing seems to fit quite right. On the car ride home Zander resumed his chatter. This time was commentary instead of questions. He thought something about the service seemed sad and not joyful. I can see that. At bedtime, when I said goodnight to Emme, she wanted to know if I was as bored as she was when I was a little girl in synagogue. I didn't want to tell her that I still feel sometimes that way in church, a place she loves and can't wait to get to every Sunday. "Yeah, I was bored then, too. Goodnight, Em."

12
DECEMBER

"TO BE A JEW IS TO BE A JEW. ITS OWN AUTONOMOUS WAY OF MOVING THROUGH THE WORLD. IT'S ANCIENT AND THICK AND VAST AND IT'S ONE SPECIFIC THING THAT IS NOT LIKE ANYTHING ELSE."

– LEON WIESELTIER.

1st Sunday in Advent. Home from church. I'm still brooding, sitting cross-legged on my bed, journaling. Tim is cheerfully busy getting all the Christmas decorations out.

"I'll be done in a few minutes!" I yell to Tim (although I know I need way longer than a few minutes to get over this state of mind). We got home from church a little while ago and he's already started today's project. All sorts of storage bins are being

JEW IN THE PEW

piled into the living room along with our nine-foot pre-lit Christmas tree that Tim bought at an end-of-season sale last year. He's still excited over the great deal he got. Tim is great at getting a deal. Everything we own has a story attached. I think it's his spiritual gifting. I, however, just need to vent a little before joining him.

We went to church this morning where I was only physically present, and counting down the minutes until we left. People seemed excited about Advent and the beginning of the beginning. This means nothing to me. I know, this is the part when Christians cock your head to the side like a confused puppy because I said that, and yet I actually am a believer in Jesus. What can I tell you? I never celebrated Christmas as a religious holiday growing up. We listened to Christmas carols and had a tree because it was fun; it had nothing to do with Jesus. I woke this morning with a feeling of grey heaviness clouding everything. On top of that, the pastor must have said the word "Christ" about 900 times. I really dislike that word. It took me years to say it without whispering it, like how people used to whisper *cancer*. It makes me think of people brandishing pitchforks and torches, shouting "Christ Killers." It still happens, that Jewish kids get called that, ya know? So stupid. Not to mention the fact that Jesus' mission was to die for the sins of the world. Make a decision, people, you want Him to die for your sins or you don't.

DECEMBER

One of our good friends is a bishop with whom I routinely spar. I suppose you could call it interdenomination dialogue except that sounds tame and it can get pretty heated. A while ago we had a conversation about that killer epithet, and my innate recoiling of the word "Christ." He just could not understand why that would still bother me. He opined that if I *really* had a relationship with Jesus, names don't matter; and no one has called me a "Christ killer" to my face. I was dumbfounded by his lack of empathy, but rallied in time to counter that, let's not forget, it is a name used as a curse word. I can't picture anyone using the word "Messiah" when swerving out of the way from an oncoming semi: "Oh Messiah! Did you see how close that truck was?" Besides that, I pointed out there are masses of Christians who don't even know what the word means. Sure, he was aware, but the majority of those in the pews think it is His last name.

Name: Christ, Jesus the.

Occupation: Savior.

I have asked a number of my Christian friends if they know what "Christ" means, and the majority didn't. "Christ" is from the Greek for "The Anointed One." Now, "Messiah" (from the Hebrew) means that as well, but it's just not a word used to terrorize Jewish children. I've heard many stories from Jews about just that happening — as a scared and confused little kid they run home to ask mom or dad who Christ is, and why are they being told they killed Him. It is a huge stumbling block to Jewish ears. It matters. It really does.

The word Messiah conjures up good feelings of being taken care of, and swooped up out of harm's way at the last moment, doesn't it? Does anyone really feel that way over the word "Christ"? Maybe. I have trouble imagining it though. It even feels harsh in the mouth to say. I rant on and on about this, because it underscores that even in verbiage the Church does not understand why it is hard to be a Jew in a church. As I said, when I am sitting in church or talking with my nice *goyishe* Christian friends, most have no idea how I feel about the word "Christ." It shows the difference between us, which makes them uncomfortable. I've seen it happen again and again. Their sideways glances, knitted brows, and a half-step back tend to give it away. They don't know how to reconcile that I am a believer but clearly not the same as they are.

Whatever. I can't change anything today. I think I'll leave all these brooding thoughts behind me and go downstairs. It sounds like Tim and the kids have put on some Christmas music. We will set up the tree with our glass, white and silver ornaments, and I'll also bring out our menorahs and growing *dreidel*[58] collection. And, you know what? It will be a lovely family afternoon.

---

58 *Dreidels are four sided tops displayed or used during Chanukah.*

DECEMBER

The holiday rush has begun. Dad has come for a visit and I finally make some real progress!

I'm standing here in my kitchen after a very long day. We just got home and I'm putting a few things away and locking up before following everyone else upstairs to bed. Looking around at the blown out candles and wrapped up leftovers I feel very proud because I did it! I finally did it! I made a beautiful *Challah*. So many times I tried and failed, but for some reason this time it worked. It tastes like the ones I remember as a kid that my grandmother would buy from Greenberg's Bakery, near City Line Avenue.

Also, an accomplishment is that I finally polished Gramom Jenny's candlesticks. Bar Keeper's Friend cleaner, $2.95. Who knew? These are the very same ones over which she would say the blessing and usher in *Shabbat*. Although I don't remember her because she died before I knew her, my grandmother tells me that I am much like my namesake. I am not exactly sure of the ways I am like her, but Gra sees it and that makes me happy. My whole life I have heard "Everyone loved Gramom Jennie and wanted to come to her house." I'm very close with my grandmother just as my mother was very close to her grandmother. It was Mom who got the candlesticks after Gramom Jennie passed away. On my

30th birthday she gave them to me because, she said, I was the one who would use them and understand why they were to be treasured.

Even though I do treasure those candlesticks, I have to admit that I've let them get a little tarnished over the years. Polishing them till the brass glowed like soft, old gold felt so good. I have often used them dull and a bit oxidized — like last month when we had company over — but it seemed disrespectful. Not to mention a telling metaphor for my state of Judaism. So, today was quite the banner day for me, what with the *Challah* victory and candlestick restoration. What progress. I am really growing as a person. Especially considering how much I had to do to get ready for Dad's visit this weekend.

Listen to everything I did. Really, it's pretty impressive. I straightened up the house, made the aforementioned award-winning-angels-singing-from-on-high *Challah*, polished the candlesticks, wiped up the downstairs bathroom, took the dog for a walk, and had my quiet time. I met my niece Gili for lunch, wrapped Dad's present, picked the kids up from school, and made a big tray of Tiramisu for dessert. All that, *and* I managed to round up Tim and the kids into the kitchen at dusk, so we could usher in *Shabbat* by lighting the candles while saying a blessing and then the *Barucha*[59] over the bread (which I made... you got that part, right?). I couldn't manage the wine

---

59 *Blessing*

however. Still, that is amazing. If only I could have a few days like that in a row I'd have to sew an "S" on my shirt.

Within moments after we lit the candles, Ellen and her four kids, Dad and my stepmother all walked through the door. I blew out the candles. Such a *shanda*[60]. You're supposed to let them burn down on their own. Then we piled in a couple cars to go to dinner at a local riverside restaurant. Okay, not ideal but still the commandment is to remember and observe *Shabbat*, and that I did. For a whole ninety-seven seconds. Perfect is just not possible because, really, whose "perfect" would it be? In our dual-heritage household, we plug in the Christmas tree lights with one hand while we light the Shabbat candles with the other.

I'm off to bed, happy but profoundly exhausted.

Taking a break from writing I decide to water the poinsettias. In doing so I accidentally spilled the water all over me, startled, I jump back and almost knock over the Christmas tree. The entire thing clinks and rattles as hundreds of clear glass ornaments knock against each other. Otis looks at the trembling tree, then me and goes back to sleep.

---

60 *Shanda is Yiddish for a shame or pity.*

JEW IN THE PEW

I decided to tend to our plants when I realized that instead of getting work done I had been shopping online for *dreidels*. Clearly my brain had enough of thinking for a while. Holiday spirit abounds around here now. The tree and decorations are up; the cards are ready to be mailed. Holiday music and TV specials have been playing non-stop: Rudolf, Jack Frost, and Tim's childhood favorite–*Snoopy's Christmas*. I wonder if that chipmunk cartoon will be shown. I didn't grow up watching these Christmas shows. Tim did of course. He has many fond memories of lying on his belly on a brown shag rug: chin cupped in his hands, feet up in the air behind him, staring at the big-cabinet TV console watching *Peanuts*, or some Claymation TV special (Oh, I bet he was cute!).

It's not that I wouldn't have been allowed to watch these programs as a kid; it's just that somehow it never happened. Yes, my dad always had a tree, but remember I lived with my mom in a very Jewish community. We never went caroling, made cookies, or bought one of those dense fruitcake bricks. I was never part of a school Christmas pageant, or had a parent risk their lives stringing lights on the roof, or owned a bright red sweater with a reindeer stitched into it. By now I have finally seen all those old Christmas TV specials that Tim loved so much. They are cute, but just don't transport me back to the wonder of childhood like they do for Tim.

DECEMBER

I am trying to make our own traditions, but it's hard with so many options between us. Tree: check. Baking: check. Christmas and Chanukah music: check. *Latkes:*[61] check. Church on Christmas: Well, check—sort of. We've gone most years, not every though. A Christmas Eve service is a beautiful thing but I still tend to feel out of place. More than any other time holidays are when I feel like an alien there - the Jew in the pew. One Chanukah tradition I started is collecting *dreidels*. There is an amazing artistic variety. I especially love the intricate metal ones, though I collect them all. Two weeks ago, I bought one online. There isn't a lot of *Judaica*[62] around me. In fact, a big clue that I am longing to be with other Jews is when I suddenly realize that I just spent an hour roaming the Internet for *dreidels*. Some people self-sooth with food or drugs, I shop for *dreidels*. A beautiful little pewter one I ordered just came in the mail. I should go put it with the others and change into a dry shirt. Maybe then I'll be ready to get back to work.

Sitting by the fire and enjoying a cup of green tea. Books are scattered around me. I'm trying to decide which one to read next. Em is working on a puzzle. Zander and Tim are

---

61 *Potato pancakes*
62 *Literary or historic things pertaining to Judaism*

playing Risk, which is apparently a friendly game of world domination.

I love these evenings when we just hang around the living room by the fire. This is the plus of living in Northern Florida; it gets cold enough for a couple weeks during the winter to use our fireplace. Last night we were wrapped in coats and gloves for our neighborhood *luminaire* walk. Everyone was outside lighting little white bags filled with sand and votive candles that had been placed along driveways and the curves of the street. My friend Amy put a card table at the end of her driveway as a pit stop for warm, spiced cider. People came by for some, chatted and then continued to stroll along; stopping in groups of people here and there to say hi to those we haven't seen in a while. It was a lovely, cold and crisp night with twinkling stars above us. We see wonderful stars here because we are so close to the blackness of the ocean, and far enough away from city lights. After an hour or so, everyone bid each other goodnight and happy holidays, and went back inside their own homes.

I enjoy my neighborhood and church communities, but I want a Jewish community too. When I was little, I had a couple of separate lives with my divorced parents, as well. This holiday was a Dad holiday, that holiday was a Mom one. Not together, and not as one big, happy family. I kept them separate in my mind so that the deep sadness didn't bleed all over the place.

DECEMBER

It was a coping mechanism. It seems I may have done the same thing with this Jewish/Christian dilemma. The ironic thing is that just as mommies and daddies belong together, I think Judaism and Christianity do also. At least more than they do now, because, ideally and like I've been saying, Christianity should embrace its Jewish roots. In the book *Girl Meets God,* Lauren Winner described the feeling of leaving Judaism for Christianity as a divorce too. Maybe spiritual belonging and identity can only be understood in family terms.

It recently surprised me to realize that in lieu of an *actual* Jewish community, I have created one out of books. The bulk of what I've been reading has been written by women with whom I would have identified and befriended in real life; women who have found themselves on a spiritual journey and who aren't afraid of forcing themselves look at things. I just found another book at the library about growing up Jewish — little vignettes, personal snapshots on paper. It makes me realize how many good memories I have of growing up in Messianic Judaism in a Jewish neighborhood and next door to my grandparents. Knowing that Gra is starting to fade I feel this great urge to carry on. When I call her on Friday afternoons to tell her of my *Challah* progress, that I am polishing Gramom Jennie's candlesticks, or just to say *Shabbat Shalom*, she is delighted. Gra tells me that it makes her so happy that I am carrying on traditions, and not letting go. Maybe this quest is not only my journey here. I am part of a vast continuum. Nothing could be more Jewish than observing *Shabbat*, and believing in the Messiah. Yet, so much of my angst exists because when I am at church, I feel that I am being so *un-*Jewish. This feeling persists even though it is *my* Messiah, too, that is worshipped at church. Something still feels amiss.

Christmas songs play in the background while I clean the house. "White Christmas" is a favorite. The composer, Irving Berlin, was Jewish. Just thought you'd like to know that.

I was just vacuuming up tiny, iridescent snowflakes that have hurled themselves off our tree, and are all over the living room floor. We may still have these things embedded in the carpet in May. Near the end of vacuuming the downstairs I realized that I had been smiling the whole time. I was thinking about our *Shabbat* a couple of days ago.

The other night, before we went to a friends' annual Gingerbread House decorating party, I made sure that we had *Shabbat*. I didn't have time to make a *Challah* so after picking the kids up from school, we stopped at the store to buy one. I also bought stuff to make Corned-Beef Specials for Saturday's lunch because in the book I am currently reading, the woman tells about her experiences growing up Jewish. Her family ate cold cuts every Saturday so no one had to cook; which, if you're Orthodox, means breaking the Sabbath. I'm not planning on being that intense but I did suddenly want a nice deli tray. Besides Mom told me that when she was growing up Gra, just like Gramom Jennie before her, did the same thing. When we got home, I cleared the dining room table of the clutter laid out for our neighborhood Christmas party. For some reason I had volunteered to make the centerpieces. I then set it with a white-lace tablecloth, on which I placed our nice plates with a thin line of gold around the rims. Emme asked if her friend Evy could eat over. "Of course!" I wish my kids would invite friends more often to share our *Shabbat* meal. It would mean they are proud of, and comfortable with, our heritage and the rituals I am instilling into our lives more regularly.

We all sat down and blessings were said over the candles, wine and bread. I felt a little like God in the beginning — I looked around and saw that it was good. We had an interesting talk and there was that soft, glowy warm, family feeling. I asked Evy if she remembered that one of the Ten Commandments says, "Remember the Sabbath." She did. "Well, that is what we are doing. We are taking time out this evening to remember God's blessings of food and family in our lives." So this week's *Shabbat* went really well and fed my soul. Gramom Jennie's candlesticks were shiny, and the way they cast the light around the table made my heart happy. I carried that feeling with me, as later in the evening we left the house to go to the Gingerbread party, Evy in tow.

The next day, Saturday afternoon, I made a Corned-Beef Special for Zan and me to share — some nice Jewish rye bread, Russian dressing, coleslaw and corned beef. The only thing missing was the pickle out of the barrel. Visions of the Jewish deli of my youth danced in my head. Zan took one bite of the sandwich, shook his head and handed it back. At first I was disappointed but then I had to laugh. Two steps forward, one step back. We did have a good *Shabbat*, but (so far) the kid would rather have a ham sandwich on white bread with mayo than the rye bread, Corned-Beef Special of his ancestors. Baby steps.

Day after Christmas. Clean up day.

"Okay, kids, finish up what you're doing and come help me in a few minutes!" Funny how if I yelled that dinner was ready they would hear me but for this I get no answer. "I'm not kidding. We are putting away all the holiday stuff today." Contrary to what you may think by packing it all up post haste, I do enjoy Christmas. And we've always celebrated it with the kids. One year, unbeknownst to us, Zander decided to decorate his bedroom. I think he was about six years old at the time. Tim and I were downstairs talking with a visiting friend when all of a sudden we heard a really horrible, grinding noise, the sound of popping glass, accompanied by the smell of something burning. Tim bounded up the steps to find that Zan climbed onto his bunk bed, and made a grappling hook out of Legos to string Christmas lights around his ceiling fan, leaving himself enough room on the wire to reach the plug. Then he turned on the fan (hoping to see spinning lights), and it quickly became a winch. Hence, the horrible grinding sounds, broken glass, and burned-out motor. Emme walked by, looked in at yet another crazy thing her brother did, sighed, shook her head and went to her room. So sure, Christmas is a total *schlep*, and sometimes you have to do a little rewiring after it's all over. That doesn't mean it isn't fun — the tree, the decorations, the carols, the TV specials, the gifts, the parties, and the lights. But still, by December 26th (which is today) I can't wait to clean up and have my living room back.

"Otis, move. I gotta put these boxes there." He dutifully jumps off the sofa and watches me start to take ornaments off the tree.

We went to church on Christmas Eve. It's nice to see everyone excited, and dressed up. But I'll confess that in all my years of being a believer, I have never felt Christmas to be a profound religious experience. Those around me seemed to be worshipping, and appeared touched. But I'm simply pleasantly watching, like a spectator enjoying seeing people in other countries enjoy their customs and traditions.

I do wonder about this colossal emphasis Christians put on celebrating Jesus' birth. I mean, on one hand God went to great lengths for Yeshua to have a humble beginning. On the other hand, He was divine, raised people from the dead, healed diseases, fulfilled prophecy, and changed the course of history. Yet, when a twelfth of the year is focused on Sweet Baby Jesus, a vulnerable, infant, it seems to deflate the impact of His power. Did I somehow miss where in the Bible is any indication that He or God wanted us to launch into elaborate spasms of celebration of His birth? It is, however, recorded that He observed the Feasts and came to uphold the law, not abolish it.[63] I certainly don't expect my Christian brothers and sisters to forgo Christmas. As I said, it's fun after all. It just makes me sad when I receive confused, almost pitying looks when I explain that Christmas just doesn't spiritually do it for me as the Feasts do. Their looks seem to say they think *I'm* the one going astray.

"Emme! Zander! I'm not kidding. It's time to put the Christmas stuff away. Come help!"

---

63 *Matthew 5:17*

Zander appreciating the candles

13
CHANUKAH

"Blessed are you, Lord our God, King of the universe, who wrought miracles for our fathers in days of old, at this season."
— One of the Chanukah blessings.

First night of Chanukah. "On the first night of Chanukah my true love gave to me..."

Even though we do Christmas presents, I also give the kids a little something on each of the eight nights of Chanukah. Just for fun, I usually hide the gifts so the kids must search for them. Though tonight I didn't for some reason. I had their Chanukah gifts on the dining room table next to an old Menorah — candles, matches and some *dreidels* that were also scattered about. But there also was a large package there that I didn't wrap. Turns out that it was for me from Tim. You'll never believe what he did.

A couple of days ago, we left the kids with my mom, and drove up to Charleston, South Carolina by ourselves for a little getaway. It had been a while and we just needed some "us" time. It's about four hours away depending on if I make us stop every hour to eat... to stretch... to find a bathroom. This drives Tim crazy, by the way. But how upset can he get when I entertain him with the update on *all* of the people in our lives, *all* the conversations I've had in that last 36 hours and then, of course, *all* of the things I'm currently worried about. Hour two is usually the time when Tim asks me if I'm going to be able to stop thinking so much, and just relax and have fun. Right. I always forget that one.

We had never been to Charleston before, and were really looking forward to it because we love charming coastal towns. We shopped on King Street — popping in and out of stores that were selling pretty things. At an outdoor market, we watched a woman make a basket out of Sweetgrass — it kind of smells like hay — while snacking on some Benne cookies. A delightful hour was spent leaning against Tim's chest in a horse-drawn carriage ride, pointing out grand antebellum mansions while listening to the *clip-clop* of hoofs that pulled us along. Although I had known that Charleston was charming, I didn't find out until we were there that it has the oldest, continuously active synagogue in America. So we went to tour *Kahal Kadosh Beth Elohim*, and learn about the building and the city's long Jewish history. It was beautiful in there and, importantly, they had a great gift shop. True to his word, Tim has stepped up to the plate and has become more interested in Jewish things. While touring the synagogue, he asked the docent questions and appreciated the history. Frankly, I got a little *verklempt*.[64]

Before we left Charleston, he snuck out to the synagogue's *Judaica* store and bought me tonight's Chanukah gift. After I opened it he asked, "Are you surprised?" It was the silver Menorah I commented on in the gift shop. "Very! How did you do this? When?" Tim was so proud of himself. "When I went to get the car when we were going to check out I rushed back over there and bought it." I had wondered why it took such a long time for him to come back to pick me up. "Thanks, Honey. You're so sweet. Let's go make some *latkes*." Note: those are potato pancakes you eat during Chanukah. It wasn't a euphemism for

---

64 *Yiddish: choked up with emotion*

JEW IN THE PEW

some other activity. Just thought I'd clear that up. Although I was pretty touched by his gift so...

The third night of Chanukah. "Rock of Ages, let our song, praise thy saving power. Thou amidst the raging foes, wast our sheltering tower. Furious they assailed us, but thine arm availed us. And thy word broke their sword, when our own strength failed us. — Maoz Tzur (Hymn)[65]

I was chiseling off some melted wax that dripped off the Menorah last night onto the coffee table while singing *Maoz Tzur* when the phone rang. Mom called. " Hi Honey. How are you, I just had the most interesting conversation with a friend whose cousin lives in...and works at...but he knows...and she said that...So it gave me an idea..." Picture all those blanks filled in with information about people I don't know whose information I'm struggling to find relevant. Twenty-five minutes later I finished cleaning off the table, dusted the living room and fed the dog all while holding the phone to my ear. But I still wasn't sure of where Mom was going with her conversation. "Mah, bullet points. Can you give me bullet points?" I've tried to explain over the years that I

---

65 *Rock of Ages, also know as Maoz Tzur, is a Hebrew hymn thought to be written during the 13th century during the Crusades. Traditionally sung during Chanukah.*

really don't need to hear each story all the back to Genesis. "Jenn, why do you have to be that way? You really need to relax. So anyway..." Once again, we are back to a friend whose neighbor has a cousin who... I take a deep breath, put her on speaker and start clean out a closet.

It turns out that Mom decided to write a Chanukah play for the kids to act out. That's a fun idea. The Feast of Dedication (i.e. Chanukah) is a great story about bravery, spiritual integrity, and resisting assimilation. In 165 B.C. the Seleucid Empire[66] dominated Judea. In an effort to Hellenize and absorb the Jews, the rulers had forbidden the Judeans to keep *Shabbat*, circumcise their sons, or study Torah. In fact, any practice that allowed worship of God became a crime punishable by death. To insult the Jews, and cause them to turn to paganism they went so far as to defile the Temple with pigs, orgies and sacrifices to Zeus.

Can I just interrupt myself here to remark on how repugnant and deeply upsetting that must have been? For you Christians reading this just imagine your church sanctuary desecrated with symbols of the occult, the cross draped in party lights and carnal activities among the pews. *That's* how bad it was.

Ok, so back to the Chanukah story.

The *Maccabees (a band of Jewish rebels led by Judah Maccabee, son of a rural priest)* had had enough and

---

[66] *Greek-Macedonian state created from Alexander the Great's conquests.*

started a revolt. After three years of successful guerrilla warfare, the *Maccabees* defeated the Syrian-Greek army and set about reclaiming the Temple. When they began to clean that gut-wrenching mess they found only one day's worth of consecrated oil for the Temple lamp, the menorah. Problem was, it would take eight days to press more of the purified oil. By some miracle that little bit lasted all eight days. So that is what we celebrate. Clearly it was also miraculous that (1) the Jews never entirely succumbed and assimilated into the greater Hellenized world, and (2) that a band of ill equipped and untrained priests fought and won against a much larger army.

So the Temple was cleaned and rededicated to God. Chanukah means dedication. Each year we gather with friends and family to light the menorah, sing songs, eat foods fried in oil and tell the story. And it seems that this year we will be telling the story via a kid's play. I wonder how Mom will address the part about the orgy. I'd call her back and ask her but I think I'd rather just wait and see. Besides, I don't have any more cleaning to do.

Eighth Night of Chanukah. Singing in the car on the way home from Grammy's: "Chanukah, Oh Chanukah, Come light the menorah. Let's have a party. We'll all dance the hora..."

CHANUKAH

"Mom, I liked your *latkes* better than Aunt Ellen's," Em piped up from the backseat. Zander expressed his agreement without looking up from playing with his new toy. "Thanks, guys. Mine are more like shredded potato and hers are the more pureed patty kind." We were on the way home from our family Chanukah dinner at Mom and Gra's house. It was a fun evening. Ellen and I had each brought our own *latke*[67] recipes to have a contest of whose were better. The kids are right, mine totally won (Sorry, El). It helped that I also made some homemade applesauce to go with them. Ellen brought that Israeli salad that she is so good at making — a skill learned during the three years she lived in Israel. After dinner, Grammy and the kids put on her Chanukah play. A cute little rendition of religious persecution, holy site defilement and an eight-day long miracle, artfully done with nine pieces of poster board, some yarn, a plastic elephant and a tiny brass menorah that Mom bought in Israel in 1974. It finished with applause from around the living room and the singing of *Maoz Tzur*.[68]

Before we opened our presents, the kids played *dreidel* with M&M's. It's really a senseless game. But it's fun to get many *dreidels* spinning at once; and if you are really talented, you can spin it upside down, on its stem. It's a show-off Chanukah move that I like

---
67 *Latkes are fried potato pancakes.*
68 *Hebrew poem sang most often at Chanukah*

to pull when I have a large enough audience. I would love to pass on the fact that Jesus often played *dreidel* as a kid every year at this time but, truthfully, He didn't. This now ubiquitous symbol of Chanukah didn't show up until the Middle Ages. But we do know that He observed the Feast of Dedication.[69] I love that it was during this celebration of God providing the oil for light and the freedom from tyranny that people came up to Yeshua pleading with Him to be straight with them, and let them know if He really was the Messiah. Clearly they were looking for a Chanukah repeat so they could get rid of their oppressors. I don't blame them. The Romans seemed like jerks. Thing is though, He just wasn't *that* kind of Messiah. Life never does seem to turn out the way you expect it.

---

69 John 10:22-24

14
FORGIVENESS & MLK

"WE DON'T RECEIVE WISDOM; WE MUST DISCOVER IT FOR OURSELVES AFTER A JOURNEY THAT NO ONE CAN TAKE FOR US OR SPARE US."
— MARCEL PROUST

New Years Day. Just finished playing chess with Zander in front of a cozy fire. Working on calendar stuff now. North Florida winters are very short. In three weeks it will suddenly be spring, like someone flipped a switch.

Today was one of those chilly days when the family huddled by the fireplace to play games, work on various projects, or hog up prime, fire-place space, like Otis does. Ever try to move a 30-pound dog that does not want to be moved? He somehow gets heavier and gives us this look like, "Seriously? Rethink that and get back to me." And back to sleep he goes. I fall for it, which Tim doesn't like. "Honey, make him move if you're cold." I'm such a sucker for my doggy though. "But look how he's enjoying it. It's ok." Otis grunts happily and rolls over to toast his other side. Tim just shakes his head and asks Zan if he'd like to play him in chess now since he beat Mommy. I would have done better but I have trouble with critical thinking when I'm chilled.

The boys set up a new chess game and Em is working on a Sudoku puzzle curled up on the sofa under a throw blanket. This seemed like a good time to update my calendar. I was wondering on what days the Jewish holidays fall this year. It's funny, I say "Jewish holidays" but really that isn't what their called in the Bible. They are referred to them as "the Lord's appointed times," or "Feasts of the Lord." It wouldn't make sense that God intended these to be merely Jewish observances because in the Torah God instructions regarding the feasts are for "you and the alien among you." The "alien among you" was anyone — *goyim* — who came alongside the Jews to worship the one, true God. How ironic that now *I* am the one who now feels like the alien in Christian circles. My, my, how times have changed. I wonder if Paul (you know, the apostle) takes a little look down from Heaven, and seeing these great holidays being ignored by our Gentile brethren, exhales a big sigh and wonders if he should have written Romans 11:17-21[70] in all caps? Speaking of Paul, I love the way he practically storms off, calling over his shoulder, "Fine, I'll just go to the Gentiles!" and then the first thing he does at any given place is go to the synagogue to worship. "Hey fellahs. Sorry I'm late. There was a mob after me and a really bad boat trip and, well, long story. I'll explain after services."

So, back to organizing my calendar — a problem that Paul did not have. The Jewish calendar is based on the cycles of the moon. Our civil calendar, called the Gregorian calendar, is not. Because these two ways of marking time do not line up exactly, it appears that the Jewish holidays are floating. But they aren't. On the Jewish calendar they are quite fixed, and have been for a heck of a long time. For example: some years *Chanukah* winds up being early in the month of December, and other years it overlaps Christmas.

---

70 *"If some of the branches have been broken off, and you, though a wild olive shoot, have been grafted in among the others and now share in the nourishing sap from the olive root, ^{18}do not boast over those branches. If you do, consider this: You do not support the root, but the root supports you. ^{19}You will say then, "Branches were broken off so that I could be grafted in."^{20}Granted. But they were broken off because of unbelief, and you stand by faith. Do not be arrogant, but be afraid.^{21} For if God did not spare the natural branches, he will not spare you either."*

JEW IN THE PEW

However, it is always begins on the very same date in the Jewish calendar, the 25th of *Kislev*[71].

The Jewish calendar has been in effect since the Exodus from Egypt. In other words, the day on which any feast is celebrated is the same date that it was celebrated 30 years ago, 300 years ago, or 3,000 years ago. So when we observe Passover on the 15th of the month of *Nisan*, we are doing it the very same date that Jesus did. Or, when we read something in the Bible that lists such-and-such happened on the fourth day of the sixth month or whatever, we know exactly what day that is on the Jewish calendar. Pretty cool, huh?

All the calendar tweaking and nice family atmosphere put me in the mood for a little nap in front of the fire. Now, if only I can move Otis just a nudge to the left...

Tomorrow morning is church again. Standing in my closet trying to figure out what to wear. I should probably just go to bed.

I don't usually plan what I am going to wear the day before but for some reason I do tonight. I'm probably just apprehensive about tomorrow since I'm

---

71 *One of the months on the Jewish calendar. For more info see back of the book.*

still thinking about last week's service. It was the first Sunday of the New Year and our pastor preached about taking stock of our spiritual lives and having new goals. He urged us to be honest with ourselves; to see if we are stagnant or have grown spiritually in the last 12 months. I have no qualms about being honest, and honestly, the whole sermon made me feel like crap. I have been doing nothing *but* taking stock and processing it, and for what? I left the sanctuary feeling somewhat numb and hung out in the lobby waiting for Tim to finish greeting people. A very nice, and rather diminutive, church lady had asked him to welcome newcomers, answer their questions, and be generally cheerful.

Tim is very good at that.

Having to be upbeat on demand stresses me out.

I could probably handle being introspective on demand, though. Or sarcastic. I could definitely be sarcastic on demand. Not really the type of thing that is Welcome-Table material. Since I am clearly not suited to join him lest I scare people away from church, I stood off to the side watching people look happy, while I felt invisible. I must not have been, though, since the pastor soon came over looking concerned. He asked how I was doing. I had been holding it together until then, but the kindness in his face broke open an emotional dam.

With tears spilling over I said, "I have been wrestling with this a long time, and for what! Where is the growth? Where is the healing? It's so hard to even come to church during the holidays!" So much for a non-informative, "Fine, thanks. How are you?" Good thing he is well aware of my heart on my sleeve personality. Though it did seem like an all-access pass to some pretty raw emotions right there in the foyer. People were walking by juggling Bibles, bulletins and coffee in paper cups, while little kids were streaming out of Sunday school with macaroni-glued Jesus pictures. Looking really confused he asked, "But why *wouldn't* you want to come to church during Jewish holidays?" I erupted: "Because I'm the only one celebrating!" I can't remember clearly but I fear I may have even added a petulant foot stamp there. Drawing on his missionary experience he offered, "Well, the Spanish celebrate their holidays and then come to church. You can still do it. It doesn't have to be an everybody thing."

By this point my passion and frustration with trying to get this message across was overflowing. "No! You aren't getting it! It is not the same. It isn't just my holiday. It's yours!" With tears unchecked I continued, and then added finger pointing for further emphasis, as if my volume and words weren't enough. "If the Church is a continuation of God's plan made of the adopted children of Abraham then we should all be celebrating together. They should know when and what holidays God set up. I shouldn't be that only one who knows it!"

At that point, Mrs. Pastor came by to remind him that he was due somewhere. If I were she, I would have used any excuse to save him from me, the ranting Jewish lunatic. Feeling abashed at my explosion, I said, "Oh, I'm sorry, I didn't mean to take you away from your job." He sweetly reminded me that this conversation was part of his job, too. Oh, right. I think I would start looking for a new occupation.

So you can see why I'm a touch hesitant to go tomorrow morning. I'm sure it will be fine. Maybe I should wear something innocuous and beige to show I'm not such a problem to have around. That is probably a better idea that the outfit built around my hot new six-inch diva heels. Hmmm.....

Martin Luther King Day. No school, which is kind of a shame because I had a lot of writing to do and now instead I'll be breaking up arguments.

"Kids, what's the problem up there?" There is a whole lot of screaming and slamming of doors. I guess I'm going to have to stop what I'm doing and see what's going on. "Mom! Zander keeps walking into my room without asking!" Or at least I think that is what Emme said. It was so high pitched and screechy as only a preteen girl can do. Right away Zander talks over her, defending himself. "Nuh uh! You are lying!" Gee, I'm so glad they have off school today. "Guys, knock it off. Em, calm down. Zan, please respect her space." They were about to launch into it again but I put my hands up like I don't want to hear it and gave them *that look*. With a cease-fire in effect I walk back downstairs to work on an article.

Before I begin I see some news about today being Martin Luther King Day and I realized that I never actually read or listened to his famous 1963 speech. You know, aside from the famous "I have a dream" clip. Quickly forgetting about the squabbling kids I was awestruck by his passion, and especially convicted when I read this:

"In the process of gaining our rightful place, we must not be guilty of wrongful deeds. Let us not seek to satisfy our thirst for freedom by drinking from the cup of bitterness and hatred."

Bitterness. Hmm. One thing my pastor said to me during my sob-fest in the lobby was, "Maybe you need to forgive the Church for its history." I've been ruminating over that one little "maybe" ever since. As I now reread King's words, there is a certain sinking in my gut. It's not that what I said to my pastor was particularly wrong — Christians should embrace their faith's rich, Hebraic roots — but he honed in on something I had been trying to ignore. For a long time I have been angry and bitter at a number of things. The first one being all the Jewish roots, expression, history and application that the Church omits. The Gentiles took my Messiah, painted Him as one of their own, removed His

"Jewishness," discarded *Shabbat* and the Feasts, and told me that I must worship Him in *their* manner. I feel thrown out of the inner courts.

The second one is the bloody history of the Church. It's so hard, as a Jew, to willingly align yourself with a group of people whose spiritual forefathers committed such heinous acts against your people over and over again. This is irrational because those people back then are *not* these people now, but it feels a little bit like a betrayal to toss your religious hat in their basket, so to speak.

I recently overheard a conversation between two Jewish (Conservative) acquaintances about this very issue. One said to the other, "Sure, the Christians are now our *friends* but who knows when they are going to turn on us again." The other guy nodded and followed up with, "Well, I don't trust them yet, either." As Benjamin Disraeli once said, "The Jews are a nervous people. 2000 years of Christian love have taken their toll." It really upsets me that Christians don't understand the depth of this wound. If I were a pastor and just met a Jew (of any persuasion — Conservative, Orthodox, non-religious, Messianic, anything) I would stand in the gap and ask them for forgiveness for the centuries of persecution at the hands of the Christians. I truly believe that it would move mountains, besides please God who aches for His people. Not to mention that it would earn Mr. Minister a helluva lot of respect from the Jew, and possibly increase Christianity's street cred. I would have found it very healing to hear it from our pastor. Instead, we have endless conversations about why this whole Jewish stuff even matters, and I get these gentle nudges about my own bitterness. Which is true... but still.

Now that I have seen these ugly things in myself, I feel desperate to go to prayer and repent. I know forgiveness is accomplished by a decision to do so, and not by waiting for the feeling. Healed emotions come later. It is like riding a bike: Your trajectory changes when you decide to turn the handlebars. Making the conscious choice to forgive is the only way to heal and stop hurting. Not forgiving is asking for the pain to dig in, like chiggers burrowing into the skin. I am heartbroken to realize that I have carried around this *drek* for so long when I have so many dear, Christian friends whom I love, respect and enjoy. I need their continued good presence in my life. I've got to go pray now and forgive the Church for how it has treated the Jews for the last two thousand years. And I better do it quickly before another argument starts between the kids.

It's a cold and damp morning. Still winter and not yet spring, though garden catalogues are scattered over the coffee table.

I keep a bowl on the kitchen counter to collect scraps for our compost pile where our veggie trash gets transformed into garden treasure. It's a metaphor for life, I suppose. We get rid of the emotional rotting lettuce left too long in the fridge, or the mental eggshells and it's reworked it into building blocks for new growth. So, in this vein, I suppose there's been progress. Forgiving the church for its bloody history and current unawareness has helped a lot. The pain doesn't seem as raw at the edges. At the beginning of this spiritual journey, I thought I just needed to know where I belonged. I figured I'd go there and then all the pain and discomfort would evaporate. But I guess that wasn't God's idea and there's more to it than that. I currently feel like a Lego creation that has been completely dismantled — tiny pieces strewn all over the floor. I can't put it back together as it was before. Nor do I want to. But neither do I know how it should be reconstructed. I kind of feel like, "Now what?" I think I will go muck around in the garden and prep things for new plants in the spring, even though I have no idea what I will plant.

Sitting at my desk reading: "Tikkun Olam is the Jewish mandate to do what we can to make the world a better place for all God's children through charity, justice and compassion."[72]

---

72 *From the website for Kesher Israel Congregation, in West Chester, Pennsylvania*

JEW IN THE PEW

I have been reading about *Tikkun Olam*, which means "repairing the world". It means doing something to help repair a fractured world. Doing for others, helping the less fortunate is a strong mainstay of Judaism (Of course it is for Christianity too. Where do you think that came from after all?) The thought is that we as God's partners on earth are meant to make a difference in kindness, help, compassion and aid. I love this idea. I love the thought of being in cahoots with God to bless someone. But the more I read, the more I am crestfallen about my life. What do I do? I write. I drive carpool. I make dinner. I garden. I am barely figuring out what to teach my kids about God, their heritage, Judaism and Christianity. And in all that, I feel as if I am doing nothing; doggie paddling to nowhere. As I chewed on this, I stared out the window. A trio of Crepe Myrtles makes a canopy overhead, birds dart in and out of leaves and flutter to the ground here and there. They must be stopping by on their migratory path. How nice that they've found a pleasant spot in our trees.

Just then a ping from my computer redirected my attention. I got an email from my thirteen-year-old nephew, Jordan. He had to write an essay in school about someone he loves, and why. He wrote about me and thought I'd like to read it! How amazing. You know, you just go along in life, doing what's been put in front of you, and desperately trying not to make a bigger mess of things and then you find out that you have made a difference in someone's life. Fabulous. I must include part of his essay.

"I chose to write about my Aunt Jenny because I feel that we can bond easily, and I feel she understands me. Sometimes when I spend the night at my cousins' house, I stay up late and talk to her about life. Our conversations can vary from simple, everyday things, to more important things like her experiences growing up, and things I am dealing with now. I love being at her house. Every time I'm there I feel safe and loved. It is such a warm and cozy atmosphere. I love how she always has a nicely made bed for me, just waiting to be slept in. I appreciate having a person like this in my life that I can go to talk to whenever I want. I hope I can be the same kind of person in someone else's life one day."

And I thought you had to be dead before people said such nice things about you.

15
NEW THINGS

"WHERE YOU ARE HEADING IS MORE IMPORTANT THAN HOW FAST YOU GET THERE."
-ANONYMOUS

Thursday. 8:50 AM. At Shelby's Cafe in Atlantic Beach where the specials are written on the huge chalkboard and sunlight streams in through the lace curtains.

I'm sitting at an eclectic beach coffee shop killing time between some appointments this morning. My chai has grown cold because I have been so busy reading, and people watching. There is an older couple sitting at an adjacent table working on a crossword puzzle. He is reading the questions aloud to her. "Six letters. Mafia Kingpin. Third letter P." She looks a little lost, but he is giving this attention like a lawyer to a deposition: eyebrows slightly raised, glasses perched, pen in hand. He moves on, "Okay, we've done that. Let's now look at number 37 down."

I turn back to the newspaper in front of me, and my eyes fall on a notice about a get-together for Jews who would like to connect with other Jews in the area — a coffee-chat type thing called Jewish Java. This looks really interesting, and it's only a half hour away from my house. "I've lived on the outskirts long enough," I say to myself. "It's time now." Excited, I start daydreaming about attending when I hear a chair scrape against the floor. The older lady has gotten up to go to the bathroom while he roots through a bag for a folding checkerboard, and a zip-top bag filled with chess pieces. How long are these people planning on being here? I suddenly realize the time and head out the door, but not before ripping that notice out of the newspaper. I really want to check it out.

Spring has sprung and new growth is just popping out of trees and plants. It's a beautiful, breezy, sunny, 70 degrees.

What a day. It's just gorgeous. I went to Jewish Java this morning and my mind is buzzing over it. I've been wandering around the yard indiscriminately pruning, and completely lost in thought. Ten minutes ago I got the loppers out from the garage. Now,

NEW THINGS

where there once was hearty 6-foot hibiscus now sits a three-foot truncated shrub, along with some other landscaping casualties. It wasn't until I was standing in a thigh-high pile of branches in front of a fairly denuded Laurel that I realized I had better put down the loppers and go write about this morning.

I enjoyed myself so much at the coffee klatch, and it felt good to be there. I had a number of interesting conversations. A variety of Jews attended: young, old, Orthodox, Conservative, Reform, and unaffiliated. We milled around with our coffee and introduced ourselves to one another, having pleasant little conversations and then moving on. Before I walked in the door, I gave a lot of thought to what I wanted out of this meeting, and how I was to present myself. My goal is simply to re-engage with the Jewish community in my area of town (sort of my area, as most Jewish things are an hour away), and not to shove Jesus down their throats. For me, yes, God has a Son and for me, yes, that Son, who the Christians call Jesus, is Yeshua, the Jewish Messiah. I gotta tell ya, I'm sooo not interested in ever being a pushy proselytizing freak with an agenda. "Normal" is a goal that people should shoot for nowadays. Actually, I don't see how the fact that I am a believer has any negative effect to being Jewish. When Lubavitcher Rebbe Menachem Schneerson's[73]

---

[73] *Schneerson died in 1994. He was a prominent Hasidic leader of Chabad. The belief that he was the Messiah still*

devotees believed he was the Messiah, no one said they were no longer Jews. Again, I could be Buddhist and a Jew, or a lesbian and a Jew, or an anything and a Jew — so I am a believer in Yeshua and a Jew. Get over it. That's my stance and I'm sticking with it.

I spoke with a woman named Robin who is Jewish but her husband isn't. After hearing a little about Tim and our life, she asked me point blank, "So, you are really raising your kids both, then?" Quick thoughts in my head: Um, yeah, I guess I am. It's not one or the other. They are both. We are both. What I said out loud: "Yes, we are." Her response was affirming, "I have to hand it to you, that's not easy. But good for you. We had to pick one. I couldn't manage both." Then she invited me to a mahjong game at her house.

Next, I found myself talking to a Conservative Rabbi with a white beard and fedora, who asked me if I'm married and where we go to synagogue. When I mentioned that my husband isn't Jewish and we go to church, he responded with a good-natured suggestion that I should come try his *church* — he all but used air quotes. I told him that our church is planning on having a Passover *Seder*[74] this year, first time ever. With a shrug of his shoulders, and tilt of his head to one side and palms uplifted he said, "Sure, but it won't be a

---

holds in some circle where they await his return.
74 *Hebrew: order. It is the ritual feast.*

NEW THINGS

Jewish Seder because they include Jesus." He said this twice, like how things are repeated in the Old Testament for emphasis. I just stood there for a minute, thinking. My emotions and my thoughts have always played across my face like a movie. I wonder if the rabbi read in my briefly knotting brows that I was thinking, "But Jesus was Jewish" But to him I said, "I think it is pretty neat that they want to learn about Passover though. Don't you?" He promptly seemed disinterested in our conversation, and moved on. I don't think it was because of the Jesus thing though — someone had just taken the Saran Wrap off a tray of *rugelach*[75] and brought out fresh coffee.

My favorite conversation was when I met the beautiful Claire. I can't tell how old she was. 200 maybe. White bouffant hair, twinkly eyes, and a set of newly bought teeth. Her posture was in a permanent, forward leaning position, and I noticed she was careful to touch something for support. We introduced ourselves and inquired about the where's, when's and who's. All that normal getting to know someone stuff, when she laid a hand on my arm to steady herself and then asked, "So, where did you get that cashmere sweater?" Delighted by this instant rapport between us, I said, "Believe it or not, Costco. Last year. $39." She nods and says, "I believe it. I'll tell you why," she

---

[75] *Jewish pastry of Eastern European origin.*

JEW IN THE PEW

says, while pointing and wagging an aged and heavily ringed finger in the air. "Last year I got a sweater for my husband there. He's buried in it. It was a lovely two-ply." She continued confidingly, as if he was about to overhear her, "You know he didn't like to get too dressed up so I wasn't sure. But it was a beautiful sweater." What a sweet little old lady. Maybe we can go shopping together sometime.

Claire also told me that when she moved to the area thirty-five years ago, she was sure that she was the only Jew in the area. "Lonely, but no trouble." She meant that no one was there to share the holidays or *kibbitz*,[76] but at least there wasn't any problem with anti-Semitism. I understood. I told her that I live half an hour south from where we were, and that I often feel the same way. "Lonely, but no trouble," I repeated to her. She was darling and nodded back at me understandingly. I liked Claire and I think Claire liked me, too.

I was about to head out the door when the organizer of the event stopped me to ask a few questions. Isabel, as it turns out, is a major connecting force in Jewish Jacksonville. Think of Barbara Streisand's character Dolly Levi in the *Hello Dolly* musical — but without the feather hats. Within moments, she told me that I should join *Hadassah*[77] and meet some other women.

---

76 *Yiddish: make comments*
77 *Hadassah is both the world's largest women's organization*

My great-grandmother (Gramom Jennie) and Gra were Life Members. Mom had been a member years ago, too. Somehow the idea just never surfaced in my mind before. Since I was now looking for a way to get more involved with the Jewish community, serve Israel, and I liked the people I met very much, I joined right then and there.

I'm still smiling from these interactions. Tim will be happy that I went and had a good time. However, he may not be as thrilled with our hacked-up landscaping. "Sorry, honey, I was a little distracted. Good news though! The coffee klatch this morning went really well! And that tree will grow some new limbs... sometime."

Sunday afternoon. Just got back from my first Hadassah meeting. I was looking forward to telling Tim about it ... until I pulled in the driveway and looked up.

---

and worlds' largest Zionist organization. They raise money for Hadassah Hospital, a teaching and research facility. It's discoveries and procedures have set the stage internationally for medical breakthroughs. Hadassah's other projects provide education for Israelis, protect at-risk children, and support the JNF (the Jewish National Fund that has planted all the trees in Israel). The organization also serves as an advocate against discrimination and anti-Semitism.

I walked in the door and asked, "Tim, are you aware of the fact that Zander is up a tree with a chain saw?" I'd have to wait to tell him about my meeting since he just stomped outside to deal with the situation. I moved on. "Hey Em, whatcha up to? Wanna hear about my meeting?" "No, not really. I forgot to tell you, there's a bunch of stuff I need for school tomorrow. We have to go to Target now before they close." Well that took the wind out of my sails. I turned around and walked back towards the door telling the air as I went, "It was fun. I met some really nice people and learned some things." The air wasn't interested, either.

We pulled back out of the driveway and away from Tim talking very sternly to Zander who was by then on *terra firma* sans power tools.

Running errands today. Life got suddenly busy. It's been weeks since I last wrote.

I happened to be doing a few errands near my mother and grandmother's house today. Since I had a spare half an hour before it was time to go get the kids from school, I called to see if it was a good time for a visit. Mom answered the phone. "Oh, hi Jenn. Of course you can come over! What kind of question is that?" Then she yells to the other room, "Mom…

NEW THINGS

Mom! Jenny is coming over... Yeah, now... No, you have time to go to the bathroom first."

This was good time to fill Mom and Gra in on how Jewish Java went, that I joined *Hadassah*, and the various other Jewish events I have since attended. I then invited Mom to go with me to a town-hall meeting. From what I heard, it will be a gathering of Jews in the beaches area. They are getting together to discuss what the community would like in terms of programs or gatherings. I thought that sounded interesting and she would enjoy meeting some of the nice people I've met. Besides, she and Isabel would probably really hit it off. Mom said she heard about it but didn't plan on going. "Why don'tcha wanna come?" Gra piped in, "Yeah, Lon, you should go." Mom said that she expected they were going to talk about how to get rid of the Messianic Jews. I was pretty surprised by her intensity. "Mah, I gotta to tell you that in the various meetings I've now gone to, it has never once come up. I think they are a lot more interested in their own lives than what a few Messianic Jews are doing." It's not so unusual for a Jew to have a slight persecution complex but to have an extra case of it from fellow Jews? Sheesh, that's bad. She gives me a serious look and says, "Listen, I'm glad you're meeting people and feeling good about this. And it makes my heart ache to not be with other Jews but I just can't go do that. Not yet."

"Okay, Mah, I hear ya." And then I had to go. It was time to go pick up the kids.

16
TEACHING MOMENTS

"THE LIVES OF FAMILIES ARE DETERMINED BY THE COMMUNITY IN WHICH THEY LIVE AND THE CULTURAL TRADITION FROM WHICH THEY COME."
— *BERNICE WEISSBOURD*

Eating some hamantaschen and on Facebook looking at pictures of friends' kids dressed up for Purim. "Aw, how sweet." I say out loud. Otis opens one eye and then goes back to napping.

Yesterday, which was Sunday, was *Purim*. In case you don't know that's the holiday that celebrates the deliverance of the Jews in the book of Esther. In synagogues, the *Megilla*[78] is read aloud and each time Haman's name is said the congregation shouts out *booo*, and often makes noise with groggers. People cheer when Esther or Mordecai is mentioned. *Purim* parties are festive and carnival-like. I remember in the synagogue when I was a little girl — kids dressed up like King Ahasuerus or Queen Esther. There was always at least one boy who dressed as Haman with a black beard, and spent the whole time trying to be evil and making us girls shriek and run away.

I wanted to take my kids to the Jacksonville Jewish Center where they were having a *Purim* Carnival in the afternoon, but there was no way we could fit that in with everything else we had to get done. So, I made adjustments and tried to bring the holiday to us. After church —where, by the way, no one had any idea it was a biblical celebration of God's deliverance — we drove an extra 20 minutes to pick up some *hamantaschen*[79] cookies. I wanted to share them with our home group that was meeting that night. Once a month we meet with a group of neighborhood families to have a potluck dinner, and have a little talk about something in the Bible. We share what is new in our lives, eat and talk while the kids play. A few families are Catholic, most are nondenominational Christian, and then there

---

78 *Entire book or scroll of Esther*
79 *A 3-cornered shaped Purim pastry*

is us. Well, it was *Purim right?* So I wasn't about to let the holiday go by without doing something. I made *groggers*[80] out of taped-up tin cans with pennies inside for the kids to shake and boo while I read the story of Esther. Afterwards, they tried the *hamantaschen* and I concluded by saying, "If it wasn't for Esther's bravery we would not be in this room together." The Catholics just stared at me. And the non-denom Christians looked like they got it until they realized that they actually didn't. "Uh, you mean, the Jews, right?" Clearly, I needed to flesh this one out for them. "No, *none of you* would be at this *Christian* home group. If God had not answered the Jews' prayers for salvation from Haman's plan of destruction then Jesus — who was *Jewish* remember — would never have been born." A look of understanding finally appeared.

Breadcrumbs. Seriously, guys, this is part of your religion too.

But back to today. Here I sit looking at these Facebook pictures. I'm glad yesterday went well at home group and they appreciated it but still I'm a bit sad that I wasn't able to see my own kids dressed up like Esther or Ahasuerus, running around a room full of other little Jewish kids who didn't need to be instructed on what a *hamantaschen* was.

---

80 *Noise makers used at Purim.*

JEW IN THE PEW

Shhhh.... everyone else is still asleep. The morning fog is still hovering. I just woke up and padded to the living room sofa to finish reading a Southern Living magazine before the house wakes up. It's Saturday so that means everyone will be home and this will be my only quiet time.

Our dining room table is still covered with last night's happy *Shabbat* dinner debris — glasses with varying levels of wine or water, crumpled up napkins, the candlesticks with the burnt-out stubs, and a few books that were talked about. Somewhere along the way, *Shabbat* has become more a part of our lives, and with fewer struggles. We had some close friends over with whom we have spent many dinners together, either here or at their house that overlooks the river. Usually, the kids want to sit at another table but for *Shabbat* I wanted everyone to sit together, by the glow of the candles to drink and eat together, to talk, discuss, laugh and create some memories. And that is what we did. I recited the blessing over the candles. Tim and Zan spoke the blessings over the wine and *Challah* in Hebrew and in English. It was a good meal, but too soon the kids were ready to pop up and go off to their own things. I made them hang around the table a little longer, explaining our (new) Shabbat tradition of discussing something about the Bible, God, and/or Jewish things.

"Ok, kids, tell me why *Shabbat* is important?" They practically answered in unison while rising from their seats to skedaddle, "It's one of the Ten Commandments." "Whoa, whoa, whoa. Sit back down. Why do *you* think it was made one of those commandments?" It took them a little while to understand that this was to be a forum for sharing what *they* think, and not just repeating pat answers. I wanted to hear their opinions, and maybe debate. What could be more Jewish than that, after all? Then we all, kids and grownups, discussed what God had in mind for *Shabbat*, the need for rest and the gift of taking time out for enjoying family. That brought us to a conversation on what it means to be holy. Zan's shouted out (remember he's loud), "It means to have something be set apart for God!" I don't think I could have said that so succinctly at his age. And I'm certain I would not have bellowed it.

We talked a bit more and then finally let the kids leave the table. They scampered away like fawns through a forest, bounding past chairs and each other. We grown-ups stayed around and finished the bottle of wine that they brought and discussed history, religion, politics, raising kids and business decisions. How blessed we are to have people in our lives to wrestle with issues and then slide into another conversation so easily. That was a good *Shabbat* dinner, and so walking by the still messy table in the morning's light makes me smile.

Maybe this is a springtime allergy. I've been cleaning and feel like I just have to sit down for a minute. I'm going to read my latest book while waiting for my tea to boil.

"Otis, you're lying on my book. Okay, I'm happy to see you too. Stop licking me. Just lay down so I can read for a minute, will ya?" Now that I've pried my book out from under Otis's *tuchas*[81], I can get settled on the sofa and tell you about it. It's the story of Eliezer Ben-Yehuda, the man who brought Hebrew back to the land of Israel in the late 1800's, before it was a State. Up until that time Jews all over the world conducted business, created works of literature, and spoke to each other in the language of their resident country and/or *Yiddish*,[82] or *Ladino*.[83] Hebrew was only used to read the Tanakh (the Hebrew Bible). However, for the most part, when dealing with anyone who was a non-Jew, they spoke the language of whatever country in which they were living. We had been dispersed around the globe for almost 2,000 years without a homeland or a common language, and yet miraculously remained a

---

81 *Yiddish for rear end, butt.*
82 *A blend of Hebrew and German for those living in Europe.*
83 *A blend of Hebrew and Spanish for those in countries surrounding the Mediterranean.*

people. With *Zionism*[84] on the rise, Ben-Yehuda moved from Paris to Israel to raise a family that would only speak Hebrew. He published a Hebrew newspaper, and founded Hebrew schools. He wrote countless articles for Jewish newspapers all over the world, arguing and defending the need for a Jewish homeland — one in which the people would speak Hebrew as their own, uniting language.

Fascinating book. His grandson of the same name is a rabbi who currently lives an hour from us. I met him a couple of weeks ago, though this book had been on my shelf unread for years. He seems to be both a kind and dynamic man, and he bears a marked resemblance to his grandfather. He told me that he is very involved with furthering relations between Jews and Christians. Maybe this grandson will be revolutionary as well. There definitely needs to be more unity and understanding between the natural and adopted children of Abraham.

Oh, I hear the water boiling. Tea's ready! "No, Otis, that doesn't mean it's time to eat. Go lay back down."

Friday. 8:30 AM. The sun is trying to poke through the clouds. Just in from a morning walk to shake off brooding thoughts. It didn't work.

---

84 *Movement for/support of a Jewish national homeland.*

JEW IN THE PEW

I wish I had an Advil. I have a headache and it's going to be a busy day. I need to run to school to help Zan's class with a project, take the kid's out to lunch since they have a half day, and drop Em back off at school for a play rehearsal. Then, Zan and I will run some errands before we return to pick up Em. That is all before our 3:00 appointment. A very nice lady from Hadassah invited me to meet her and some other moms at a park for their monthly *Shabbat* playgroup. My kids are really too old for that, but I figured that we could stop by on our way home for half an hour — an hour tops — and my kids could help with the really little ones. I was told that someone brings *Challah* and juice, they say a *barucha*,[85] the kids play and the mom's talk. Most of the women there have a spouse who isn't Jewish, but they want to get together and do something Jewish for/with the kids. Obviously I get that. When I told the kids about today's plan they reacted badly. Just to get out of it and be pissy as only preteens can, Kid #1 spit out, "Why does it even matter, it's not like I even care about being Jewish." Kid #2 stood by nodding in agreement, clearly picking up on the plan that complaining was their way out. It almost worked because I felt really defeated. As a Jewish mother, my job is to teach them who they are, their history, what we do, and why; use a little guilt when necessary to

---

85 *Blessing over the wine.*

get things done, and when they are sick make chicken soup. All I could think was, "I've failed."

Dejected, I silently went upstairs to my bedroom and shut the door. Sadness washed over me. The kids were probably hi-fiving each other and stifling a "Yesss!" After a while Tim came up, and softly closed the door behind him. As always, he was encouraging. "Don't listen to them. Kids will say anything to get out of something. This is important to you. Just go." Then he went back to the kitchen to give them a little talking to before their ride came to pick them up. After I heard them go, I went for a beach walk to collect myself before our busy day. I'm not sure I feel a whole lot better but I did find some sea glass. I know it once had sharp corners but all the sand and churning has made it into this beautiful soft aqua piece, its edges are soft and there's just something lovely about it. I think I'll carry it in my pocket today and we'll see what the day holds.

Later the same day...

The *Shabbat* playgroup went really well. I had such delightful conversations with the other moms. All of them had little kids younger than mine, but Zan was great and played with the small boys, making sure they stayed in bounds and feeling like a big kid himself. For quite a while, Em was very sweet and tried to coax a shy three year old to play. The little girl was unable to be enticed though, so Em went to the car to talk on her cell phone, which was okay – she tried. I must say that I was euphoric by the time we left the park. We got in the car to drive home and I couldn't help but say out loud what was going on inside. "I feel great. That felt great. I'm so happy." Glancing to Emme next to me and then to Zan in the back seat I saw that they seemed happy too. "Well, guys, whaddya think? Did you enjoy that *at all?*" They admitted they had a good time being the big kids, seeing the little Jewish faces, and doing a Shabbat thing. I even heard a mumbled, "Thanks for making us go." The car soared home after that in a ray of sunshine, and I think music played from somewhere up above.

I took the piece of sea glass out of my pocket and placed on the dashboard.

17
SPRING BREAK & MY BROTHER

"YOU HAVE THE CAPACITY TO CHOOSE WHAT YOU THINK ABOUT. IF YOU CHOOSE TO THINK ABOUT PAST HURTS, YOU WILL CONTINUE TO FEEL BAD. YOU CAN'T CHANGE THE EFFECTS PAST INFLUENCES HAD ON YOU ONCE BUT YOU CAN CHANGE THE EFFECT THEY HAVE ON YOU NOW."
— GARY MCKAY, P.H.D.

Sunday. Still recovering from a crazy weekend. One of my favorite sayings is that we see things not as they are but as we are.

On Saturday afternoon I opened my email to find a vitriolic letter from my brother to my mother – he cc'd my sister and me. Rick is still angry with Mom for becoming a Messianic Jew thirty-five years ago and, in his view, dragging us down with her. He is six years older than I, so his youth and mine barely have much in common. Even the parents he knew are not the parents I knew. My brother's childhood was spent in the years before the divorce, when the family was whole, living in the suburbs, and everyone went to the Reform synagogue together. But a significant chunk of my childhood was after the divorce, spent in Philadelphia, when Mom got really involved with Messianic Judaism and Dad was non-stop involved with his work. I'm not sure what exactly set him off and prompted this email, but somehow I got in the middle of it. Rick wrote that I have no idea what it is to be a real Jew because I never read anything Jewish (my bookshelf proves otherwise), I never hang out with Jews (I'm not sure how the *Hadassah* ladies would feel about being told that), and I will have Gentile descendants (That one does bother me, but I did marry Tim).

I was really hurt by his words. He judged me so viciously without knowing what my life really is like, with whom I spend time, or what I read. Rick lives a thousand miles away in New York and rarely comes to visit. I wrote back and told him to knock it off, to stop being such an antagonistic ass, and come for Passover next month.

Mom, whom his invective was most intended to hurt, wrote him back. Boy, when you get her going; I had to scroll down like five times. The two of them can verbally spar for hours. In between all this family drama was Emme's birthday. So, instead of reading through all of Mom's email, I turned the computer off and hopped in the car to take Em and six of her girlfriends to an event that was an hour away, through unfamiliar territory at rush hour, in the driving rain. To make matters worse, Emme insisted she be allowed to crank up her new favorite music: Country, and one girl was a shrieker: "My dog died, my truck won't start, I'm settin' on the front porch 'til my woman comes home…" Another girl had doused herself with enough perfume to be a biohazard. I had to have the window open a bit just so I could breathe. Unfortunately, this meant being pelted with the rain whooshing off the other cars as we all hurled down I-95. Good chance Em will forget this particular birthday in the hazy remembrances of childhood. I can assure you, however, I will not.

The next morning I checked my email, and by this point my sister had joined the conversation. Ellen, ever the sweet one, finally had enough and let our big brother have it. (By the way, I love it when she *finally* gets upset! I always think: It's about damn time.) She told Rick that no matter what life hands you, at some point you need to stop moaning what your family did or didn't do, and move on. She went on to say that he was the one being intolerant and sounding religious, and that I may be more Jewish than all of us: "I bet you didn't even know that Jenny takes the kids to synagogue, teaches them about Jewish stuff,

JEW IN THE PEW

has *Shabbat* dinners, and is getting involved with the Jewish community even though she lives far away!"

I know Rick feels that Messianic Judaism robbed him of having a "normal" Jewish family. I get what he means but really *it* didn't rob him. The divorce did. Judgments about people, and what they believe, robbed him. It was misunderstandings and individual human shortcomings that failed him. In the end my brother apologized for coming across as such a jerk and letting his pain and frustration get the better of him. Sometimes we just don't see how our pain, frustration, and bitterness have become an overreaching thing in our lives until someone points it out to us. I love that by the time it all played out Rick felt cared for. He wrote back to all of us that, "Only people who really love you will fight it out, tell you honestly that it's time to deal with your crap, and still want you to come visit." I really hope he does come home for Passover. I love him and wish we were closer.

Happy birthday to me, happy birthday to me, happy birthday dear Jenny...

Tim and the kids gave me some pots of lavender and geraniums for my birthday. So today I was outside deciding where to plant them and having a lovely time in the garden when Tim brought my phone out. "It's your brother." I tucked the phone between my shoulder and ear. "Hey little sister. Happy Birthday!" It's so nice, he never forgets. Dad does. Mom does. But Rick always calls. "Hey Rick. Whatcha up to?" I like to weed while on the phone and began to work in between the pink and white impatiens under the big oaks. After I finished up there, I moved on to deadheading the irises and roses. After we talked for about 20 minutes I was about to get off the phone, thinking the conversation had run out, when he asked me a question. "In what ways are you raising your children similar or different from how you were raised?"

His therapist had recently asked him this and he wanted to know how I would answer it. I looked though our French doors into our living room where the kids were sitting and thought about the answer. I could see Tim crossing the living room with a board game in hand. Their lives are so different than mine was. I was raised in Messianic Judaism with weekly Shabbat services, Jewish holidays, and hung out with other Jews, the language we studied in school was Hebrew, and the kind of history we learned included Jewish history, the Holocaust, the birth of Israel, etc. My kids, though, are being raised more Christian, and I have to wedge in the Jewish part. What a crappy situation.

You know, I mourn the loss of all those years raising my kids differently from how I was raised. I couldn't really give Rick an honest answer there. Can you imagine if I told him all those thoughts that just went through my head! My brother can be very loving but that would be like handing him ammunition to tell me how I've failed as a Jew. Which is pretty ridiculous when you think about it because Tim and I have this great marriage and family life — something my poor sibling doesn't have — but I'd be the one who screwed up.

Instead, I just answered him something benign and told him that it was a great question and that I'd have to give that some thought. I was really happy he called though and we said I love you before getting off the phone.

After that, I allowed myself a birthday gift of spending another hour planting, thinking and puttering in the back yard by myself. This is my retreat where I go to reorient myself. A six-foot, white, privacy fence and tall trees make this a secret garden. Over the years, Tim and I have created multiple sitting areas, a pond where our Fantail Koi weave and glide between the papyrus and lily pads, a raised vegetable garden, and borders of hydrangea, camellia, milkweed, lantana and rosemary.

And I think I just found the perfect spot for my new plants.

Zander helping me at the Seder

18
PASSOVER

"THE REAL VOYAGE OF DISCOVERY CONSISTS NOT IN SEEING NEW LANDSCAPES BUT IN HAVING NEW EYES."

– MARCEL PROUST.

Full day planned. Getting ready for Passover is the ultimate Spring-cleaning for your kitchen.

Tim is at work, the kids are at school, I've cleared my schedule of other things and I am about to commence cleaning. It feels like music from the Rocky movie or something should begin. Maybe I should stretch or do a few warm ups. Feel free to picture me: I've got my hair up in two pig tails, and I'm wearing my purple rubber gloves, a tank top, jean shorts and my big frumpy slippers. Oh yeah. Game on.

A very big part of Passover is abstaining from anything with yeast in it. Before the holiday begins you remove all the bread products and various leaven from the house. But throwing out a lot of food seems wasteful, especially if you are a big cracker-loving-bread-eating-muffin-baking kind of family, like us. Long ago the Rabbis came up with a splendid idea to circumvent that feeling of guilt — sell or give your *chametz (leaven)* to some nice *goy*.[86] I really doubt that would fly with the half a cake on the counter, and my Muslim neighbor down the street though. It's probably best if I just eat the rest today before the kids come home.

Last year, I went through all the cupboards and drawers and put all the *chametz* on an inconvenient ridiculously high shelf. I was sure that was great idea until the pointy edge of a box of crackers fell on my head and put a divot in my cranium. I'm hoping this year it goes a little better. It's always a low point when you are trying to teach your kids something about God, and wind up holding your head as expletives fly out of your mouth.

---

86 *Hebrew: Gentile*

I was telling the kids about a *chametz* kit I saw advertised that contained a feather, a wooden spoon, and a written out blessing. One is supposed to use the feather to sweep out the last crumbs in the cupboard onto the spoon and burn it while reciting the blessing. But I just don't see how torching a wooden spoon in the kitchen is ever a good idea. Zan was very excited about this idea because he loves to burn things. I could just imagine coming home to a charred stump of a house because Zander decided to practice a little *Chametz* burning on his own. Besides, I didn't feel the need to spend $12.95 plus shipping and handling for a feather and wooden spoon.

All right, well, enough of explaining, I'm going back to my cleaning.

Rereading Exodus. I love this story.

Pesach[87] my favorite Jewish holiday but I can't pinpoint why. There are no presents, there are hours of cooking to be done, the meal has a long liturgy attached to it (unless you are with my family who has no attention span whatsoever), and then there is a week to go without bread, pizza, or the like. And as you've already seen, there is a lot of cleaning involved.

---

87 *Transliteration of "Passover"*

Sounds like fun, right? The thing is Passover is the defining point in Jewish history. It's when God carved us out as a nation and put His stamp on us. He refers to it over and over again in the Bible. The rescue from slavery, and that we were given our instructions for interactions with God and each another was pivotal. Not just for our history as a people, but in the *world*. There simply were no monotheistic nations on Earth prior to that point. Even to this day, our civil laws are based on Jewish law. Do not murder? Repayment for wages lost due to injury? It's all Torah baby. Besides, I love how dramatic the story of Passover is. I rewrote it... take a look. Go ahead, get popcorn, call the kids in, gather 'round.

It starts out bleak and dismal. No hope for those oppressed. One born in poverty is destined for greatness. By the boldness and ingenuity of his gutsy mother and older sister he is saved from death and instead taken to the palace, a rags-to-riches story. Time drags on for downtrodden until the one day when that very same boy, now a man and a prince, realizes who he is. Succumbing to a fit of rage he is banished and neither royalty nor slaves want anything to do with him. Only animals in the desert accompany his days. After decades of exile God appears to him.

Why him? Why now? Obediently, he returns to face those who scorned him, who have the power to kill him. He goes to ask the impossible, claiming to be backed up by a God more powerful than all their

PASSOVER

many gods. Marching into the palace, he faces off with the bad guy, a despot with a black heart. It's quite the battle. God and Moses attack the very things Pharaoh holds dear. Plague after horrible plague is directed at the Egyptian gods — the Nile, the frogs, and everything that the Egyptians worshipped. It is looking so much worse with nothing better in sight. The enslaved people wait every day to hear the news; they make their bricks with baited breath, waiting … waiting. It rages on for days, weeks, until eeriness falls over the land bringing death in its wake. In his profound grief, the king finally relents.

The Hebrews think that is the end of it, and rush to get out of that God-forsaken land. You think the story is over. But like a horror movie when evil makes one last grab, the treacherous king sends his hordes of solders thundering down upon the escaping multitudes. Running, they look back over their shoulders, terrified. Babies cry as they are held too close and jostled too much. Animals, feeling the tension in the air, buck and pull away from their restraints. The people look to their leader, who is spent and wrung out. Moses turns to God for his marching orders once again.

The impossible keeps happening in this saga. This time the sea parts leaving land dry enough for hundreds of thousands of people and wheels and animals to walk and ride on, un-mired. Even more miraculous, as the last one gets across, and as the Egyptians are almost at

JEW IN THE PEW

their heels racing through this odd ravine, the mighty sea swallows them up, obliterating the most powerful army on the face of the planet.

Imagine the faces of those astounded people on the other side. They are standing at the banks, chests heaving from the race across, mouths agape in shock at what they just saw. There is stunned silence. The sea has turned quiet once again. The Hebrews look on, the bodies of their evil oppressors floating dead in the water, and there is only the sound of gentle waves lapping the shore. And then, the roar of thousands. The relief, the praise, and the joy all escaping their lips at once:

Praise God!

Whew! Come on, now. Admit it. That was great. Oh man, I'm pumped. I think I'll go take Otis for a walk by the river. Where's my staff? Not that I'm expecting anything but you never know.

Eight AM. I'm back at Shelby's Coffee shop, sitting at an outside table waiting for Ellen.

I just dropped the kids off at school, drove over the Atlantic Blvd. Bridge, and I'm now waiting for Ellen to meet me for a cup of coffee and a bagel. Later today, Tim and I have a meeting with our pastor to talk about a church Passover *Seder*. It's great that the

PASSOVER

church leadership now wants to teach about Passover, and that so many Christians want to participate and learn about it. The impression I got, though, is that they want *us* to lead the *Seder*. I don't want to do it. Don't get me wrong, I absolutely want it done. Just by someone else. We've actually led *Seders* before at the kid's school, or at home, of course. But, you see, that wasn't where we go to church every week (or in my case, sort of go every week). I think I already feel my heart pounding a little. Maybe this is just some social anxiety. Oh good, Ellen is here. She can take my pulse. And she brought Jordan with her. How nice. I guess he has off from school today for some reason. The kid could use a nice bagel, he's looking a little on the thin side. Anyway, I shouldn't worry. We'll see what happens this afternoon. Maybe we won't even be asked.

Hours later that same day…

They asked. And, like a pushover, I agreed. But–get this–they don't want it during Passover. Seriously, I'm not making that up. They want it done during Holy Week (between Palm Sunday and Easter), which is a full three weeks *after* Passover this year. If you're getting the feeling that I'm a bit bent, you're right. I considered their insistence to *only* do it this way reminiscent of Replacement Theology.[88] I'm going to assume that you, dear reader, don't know what that is. So I'll tell you. Way back in the fifth century John Chrysostom, an early church father, wrote texts saying that it was the Christians' duty to hate the Jew, this lead to centuries and centuries of Christian anti-Semitism. The Inquisition and the Holocaust would not have been possible without his thought that Jews were inferior, dismissible, and a plague to those of "superior" stock. And it got worse. Or maybe I should just say it got more complicated because around the same time St. Augustine wrote *City of God*.[89]" It said the Gentile Church replaced Israel in God's eyes because the Jews of the first century missed the mark. Hence, it surmises, all things Jewish things must be expunged from Christian practice lest there be spiritual defilement.

I'm not making this up! It's true and it just makes me apoplectic. God's plan started, includes and ends with the Jews, because that is what the Bible says. The Gentiles are the ones to come alongside, not the other way around. And let me tell you, it's not as if I haven't had this conversation with pastors, priests, rectors and bishops before, because I have. Although, I confess, sometime during the conversation I'm

---

88 *Also called Supersessionism.*
89 *Written in 413 A.D. or C.E., whichever you prefer. I actually don't care which form is used. Isn't that refreshing?*

usually fantasizing about sweeping everything off their desks, jumping on top and yelling that what I am saying really matters not just to their flocks, but also to God. Ok, well, maybe not the guy with the glass tabletop, but the rest with those big oak desks. No one would take me seriously if I fell through on my butt. I don't know, there's a good chance they may not take me seriously now.

Did I forget my point? Oh yeah. My point is that I truly believe the Christians sitting in church — if given a chance — would like to be taught about Passover when Jesus celebrated it, according to the Hebrew calendar and God's timeline that started at Mt Sinai. Just as I was about to launch into a speech about how the things of God should not be conveniently shoehorned into a papal-based calendar the pastor explained that since this was to be the church's first *Seder*, it just made sense to do it at this time *this* year. "Oh. I see." Tim gives me this hard look that says, "You want to calm down now?"

Okay, okay. I'll calm down. The fact that they want to learn about Passover is great. Maybe I shouldn't have had that third cup of coffee this morning. Note to self: Switch to decaf.

Passover. Day One. I finally got a minute to sit down. Everyone will be here in an hour.

JEW IN THE PEW

I'm looking forward to our family Seder tonight. It feels like I have been cooking and cleaning forever. It's all worth it: I have made the best chicken soup of my life. I added some diced leeks and sautéed them with the celery and carrots in just a little olive oil before starting the soup. I can't wait till everyone tastes it.

With my in-laws visiting this year, there will be sixteen of us. Since our dining room is more bistro than banquet we've moved furniture out of the living room and set up long tables there. Picture the last supper but with a better ending to the evening. The table is now set with yards of white tablecloths, and the light blue, seventy-year-old china. Posies of deep purple and yellow violets cut from the garden this morning dot the spaces between everyone's place setting. Gramom Jenny's candlesticks are in front of my seat waiting to be used for the blessing. They look extra shiny tonight, as if they know its *Pesach*. Set at intervals along the table are the other Passover elements: the *Seder* plate,[90] matzo,[91] *charoset*,[92] bowls of salt water,[93] and parsley.[94] I needed to make room at

---

90 *The Seder plate is a special plate laden with symbolic food used during the ceremony.*
91 *Matzah is the yeastless bread also known as the bread of our affliction.*
92 *Charost is a mixture of fruit and nuts that symbolize the mortar used to make bRicks in slavery.*
93 *Salt water represents our tears shed in Egypt.*
94 *The parsley is both a symbol of the hyssop used to paint*

PASSOVER

the table for one more thing: my laptop. Rick wanted to be with us but couldn't fly down from New York, so we decided to videoconference him in. I think he is going to say the prayers over the wine and then head on out, as his rabbi invited him to his house this year.

On each plate sits a *Haggadah*, which is a small book that contains the Passover story, prayers, songs and liturgy that is followed during the *Seder*. I happen to have written this one. There have been thousands of versions created over the past two millennia. I thought it would be a nice project to compile one that suited our family. Honestly, it can't be too long because we have the ADD Passover *Seder* (i.e. five different conversations happening on eight different topics, none of which ever come to completion).

One year, when we were about to read the account of the Exodus — and keep in mind this means telling two tables of talking people, all of which are hungry and prone to smart remarks, to turn to page 20 and actually listen — Emme asked, "Can't we just put on the *Prince of Egypt* movie instead?" Everyone cracked up. It took another 15 minutes of discussion until we got back on track. And even though we know how important this holiday is and we try to get through without major interruptions, there is always one kid who just sort of wanders off somewhere. This causes a great amount of yelling from the grown-ups to get him back to the

---

blood on the door post and also used to dip in the salt water.

table. I have no idea how observant families have *Seders* that require everyone to sit at the table, hungry and yet paying attention, for *hourssss*... I'm lucky if our family will hang in there for 35 minutes. And that is with interactive snacking. "Here guys. Food. See the food? Tell me what this represents and you can have some. Shiri get back here. Ellen, where is she going? Oh man, not again."

It's moments like this that give you even more respect for Moses leading people like us *anywhere*.

The interesting thing is that even though there's a lot of work and ceremony in place (more or less), it makes us all very happy. Even the kids who aren't paying attention will mention later how much fun they had. Good chance most of the conversations down at the kid's end of the table will be reminiscing over the time which cousin, or sister or brother did what, when. In observing this tradition, we feel connected to the past, each other, and to God. Now, that the table looks so wonderful, and the food smells so good I wonder when everyone is going to get here already.

You know what else I wonder? I wonder about Jesus' Passovers. He celebrated it his whole life. As it is weeklong, that means 231 days of His time on earth was spent in observance. I wish I could have seen Him enjoy his family and friends at Passover, telling Exodus from His perspective, maybe laughing at a good joke someone made. Or at the last supper: Imagine watching Him relish His last day with His talmidim,[95] a look of love crossing His face, knowing their time together was drawing to a close. Never again would they be under the stars, talking late into the night, or trekking though the countryside teaching and ministering to people.

When He was younger, did He help make long benches for a big family Seder, like my great-grandfather did? Yeshua had a lifetime of memories of Seders: The women in the family bustling around and cooking. The men carrying items for them, or sitting around having a good debate. Family coming together from far away, their arms filled with foods, offering a relative a cheek to be kissed as they hurry on in. Nieces, nephews and young cousins chasing each other, weaving their way between groups of talking adults and getting yelled at to slow down "Hey Yakov, Yossi enough with the running already. Come help. We're about to begin."

Was Yeshua the fun uncle who always had the little nieces and nephews climbing all over him? I bet He was.

Just as I was lost in this daydream the door banged open. Family and noise poured into the house. Mom was helping Gra through the doorway while yelling at Jordan to come take the green beans from her. Ellen came in talking to me and to two of her daughters at the same time, "Jenny, where do you want me to put this? Shiri, I'm not going to discuss it again. Gili,

---

95 *Hebrew: disciples*

JEW IN THE PEW

why did you say yes?" Tim, Zander and his dad came in from the garage where they were discussing a new idea for building built-in seating for the bay window. Emme grabbed her BFF cousin Libi, Ellen's youngest, and they started to race upstairs. "Nu uh, you two! We are gonna start soon. Don't disappear."

Just wait till they taste my soup.

Writing in bed about our wonderful evening out. I'm happy.

Tonight, one of my *Hadassah* friends invited us over for the second night of Passover. She had thirty or so people and their kids over for Second *Seder*. In all my years of having *Seders* with my family and friends, I have only done the first night. Many Jews have two *Seders*, especially the orthodox and Conservative. Due to the time difference outside of Israel, this ensures the holiday is observed correctly. The practice probably stems from long ago, before the invention of atomic clocks and figuring out time zones. It does seem a little extraneous now. However, we were excited to be invited because it was an opportunity to hang out with new friends and continue *Pesach*.

I adored seeing all the little Jewish children with luminous dark eyes, many with dark hair hanging in waves or curls. I know, that's stereotypical. But they reminded me of when I was growing up. It a change from the leggy, blond hair, blue-eyed children I see predominately at church all the time. Want to hear something strange? It occurred to me tonight that I rarely feel frumpy when I am around other Jews. I can't tell you how many times I have felt like a short, little peasant with a hunchback at church where so many women tower above me, with their long limbs, tiny noses and (naturally) blond manes. I realize that's pretty insecure. What can I say? Sad but true.

Before the *Seder* began, I glanced over at Tim who was sitting with some of the other men, talking and wearing a yarmulke. He looked like he fit in and was at ease. In fact, he had a very good time. I am blessed he likes these new friends of mine, and their husbands, as much as I do. It amazes me that after years of praying, that God has answered and I now have a handful of lovely Jewish friends outside of my family. I hope to have them over for dinner soon, my sign of all those truly initiated into my world.

19

EASTER

"TO CHANGE FOR OTHERS IS TO LIE TO YOURSELF."
— MONA LISA MOVIE, 2003

Low tide and 75 degrees out. It's Spring Break. I'm at the beach with the kids. Zan is skim boarding, Otis is sniffing, ears flapping in the breeze and Em is stretched out on a towel reading a book.

I'm not sure how I feel about the book Emme is reading. It's some sort of chick-lit romance novel. Why can't she still be reading *Little Women?* There's nothing like a good romance story though. I brought that up last week at church before we started our Seder. You're probably worried I said something odd or inappropriate (which knowing me is a valid concern) but, really, this one made sense. I figured it's one thing for us Jews to embrace Passover but I thought it would be a good idea to explain why it's relevant to the Christian. Here's what I told them:

"I want you to think back on the time when you became a believer. Someone held the story for you. At the right time in your life you heard a prayer, read a book, had a discussion or heard a sermon of how God sees you and how important you are to Him. The Jews were the first to hold this story. Every year, Jews all over the world retell the dramatic rescue from slavery and the beginning of our relationship with God in first person. "It happened to me. I was a slave and now I'm free"

What you may not realize is how this is your story too. Passover is important because it is our anniversary. Just as we treasure something a loved one has given us in memory of a special time — a ring, a picture, a gift — the Seder does the same thing. Each element represents a piece of our timeline together.

When Jesus celebrated Passover and he looked around at the dear Jewish faces that had been by His side, he didn't just see them. He looked past them into the future and saw *your* face. When He lifted the cup of wine and broke the matzoh and said, "When you do this..." He was speaking that *you* would do Passover and see Him in it. At that moment Jesus was "the Word that became flesh." But understand that means that He had also been on Mt Sinai as the WORD

EASTER

giving the instructions to Moses that it was His desire that we should always remember this anniversary of God drawing us out.

It is not just first person for the Jews. Passover is the beginning of your story too. It does not make you Jewish to celebrate it and you do not need to do it as the Jews do — but I encourage you every year at this season to observe and remember the Passover. God wanted us to never forget the beginning of our relationship with Him and how he drew us out while we were still slaves. I can't imagine a spiritual walk without Passover."

Then we went on to lead them through the rest of the *Seder*. The truth is that even though I didn't want to do it, it turned out fine and all the things I worried about didn't happen. Tim keeps pointing out to me that since that always happens maybe I shouldn't worry so much. One of things that I was concerned about was that it would be weird afterwards since not *everyone* at church knew I'm Jewish. It was like coming out of the closet. I once had a Catholic neighbor tell me that I was the first Jew she ever met. Seriously. She just stared at me. At least she didn't ask where my horns were. Thankfully, no one has since has reacted like that.

I am sure that my apprehension was just ghosts in the closet — those fears that come out to haunt you from times gone past. The reality doesn't exist anymore; it is only the shadow of what was that lingers. And no one else even sees it. When I had to leave my little Jewish world and go to a Christian high school I felt like everything was so odd, so different. My classmates all seemed blissfully unaware there were *any* holidays that celebrated how God saved Jesus' ancestors from annihilation. They had barely a clue of what a Jew was, what that meant, or why it mattered. I remember sitting in Bible class and being very confused why the teaching was *all* New Testament. Why were they not taught the other two-thirds of the Bible? Why didn't it all go together? And why didn't anyone debate and have discussions? So, anyway, I just didn't know what to expect after this *Seder* at church.

But they were very sweet. Even though I firmly believe that these feasts and observances belong to Christians as well after 1,700 years of dismissing, discounting and rejecting Jewish ties to their own faith left me taken aback when they told me that they felt honored to have this shared with them. One man came up to me the other day and said that it made him think differently all week and brought new thoughts to his mind about his relationship with Jesus. That meant a great deal to me. It's not easy to try to show someone you have a piece of their puzzle, when they've been assured their picture was complete. I don't know that man's name, but I won't forget the moment. I gave out the little *Haggadahs* that I wrote for my family, too. They must have loved it because they snatched them up, every last one. And come to think of it, I never once had to bribe them with food to get them to listen.

Just got back from grocery shopping. Easter candy, bunnies, plastic eggs and baskets were everywhere. Did you know that in 1953, it took 27 hours to create just one Marshmallow Peep? Today, only it takes six minutes.

My first introduction to Easter was when I was about six or so. My mother had become a believer the year before and solemnly gave me a little Easter basket. I was completely confused by it. Six is old enough to be surprised when a holiday you never heard of pops ups. I was standing at the bottom of the stairs, the wide-plank hardwood floors beneath my feet, soft spring sunlight shone in through the sidelights from the front door. I remember feeling very little at that moment. I have no idea where my father, brother or sister was. I just know they aren't in the memory, it's only my mother handing me a basket. I looked at the stuffed white bunny and candy inside and then looked back up at her questioningly. She said, "It's for Easter," then turned and walked off to the kitchen. Whatever this new holiday was about, it didn't seem to make mom happy; she seemed downright mournful. Maybe this was about the time her marriage to my father was falling apart. Easter didn't appear again in my world until I was engaged and went to Easter dinner at Tim's parents' house.

Everyone was dressed up — stockings, heels, ties, dress pants, the whole thing. They had an Easter egg hunt for Tim's one little nephew, while some old hymns played quietly on the radio in the kitchen. Even the food was a cultural shift for me: Ham, a salad made from apples, celery and mayonnaise on small plates lined with lettuce leaves, white potato rolls, and a Jell-O dessert. Tim had fond Easter memories growing up, as I'm sure every good little Baptist boy does. When we got married he had this crazy idea that we would go to church on Easter morning. Imagine that. For years, he went and I stayed home.

With the exception of that random forlorn basket, we *never* celebrated Easter growing up. I realize that most Christians can't comprehend why Messianic Jews, who are believers in Yeshua, don't celebrate Easter. The simplest answer is they don't observe any extra biblical holidays created by Gentiles centuries after Yeshua came. They celebrate Feasts detailed in the Bible, the same ones Yeshua celebrated. Honestly, everyone else would be too if it hadn't been for some 4th century (Gentile) bishops who decided they had to get *"their"* religion about Jesus away from those damned Jews. And poof! Easter becomes a Christian High-Holy Day mandated to all believers instead of Passover. Bummer.

EASTER

The first time I ever went to an Easter service, I was 29 years old. I would not have shown up at all, except I had created some artwork that our friend Geoff, an Episcopal priest, was using in his service and I was helping plan a few things. The day before the event, I popped in to check on the placement and casually mentioned that tomorrow should be interesting since I'd never been to an Easter service before. He *s l o w l y* turned his head to look at me as if I had just said I like to sell crack to children. I have since found out that pastors don't take it well when you mention a disinterest in Easter. And if they already think you are a believer it really screws with their head. I've actually been to services a few times since then but it just freaks me out. The clergy processing in with flowing robes, cross held high aloft, and that heavy drumbeat going on. Anyone else thinking Crusades here? Just me? By the time the last stanza finishes and the confetti cannon goes off, I am just about ready to call, "Check please!" Another thing I find so disarming is the crosses —— so ubiquitous with Easter. The tradition of taking a happy family picture in front of a trio of crosses simply boggles my mind. Hello? It was an instrument of torture! And Jesus was not the only Jew who was murdered that way. Thousands and thousands of Jews were crucified. And let's not forget that Nero liked to nail up Christians, as well. I ask you, if the Romans had used guillotines would the Jones family be posing in front of a framed out angled blade with little Suzie in her new Easter bonnet? It's seriously perplexing, if not downright creepy. Look, I get it: Jesus is risen, and that is way cool. I am a believer so I do understand how profound it is that He conquered death. But the whole thing is just too much, I'd much rather stay home and maybe eat a few Marshmallow Peeps, after all they only took six minutes to make.

Easter Sunday. It's almost 2:00 pm. I only just got out of bed.

I didn't go to church this morning. I'm kind of sick. I mean, my nose is runny and my head feels like it weighs 200 pounds. I could have physically gone, although God knows I didn't want to. Last night I prayed, "Dear God, please work it out so I don't have to go. Or change me so I want to. But, mostly, the first one." I seriously did not want to go to church, but I would have if Tim had told me that it was really important to him. I would have put on an appropriate pastel-like dress, forced a smile, and then stood or sat, while everyone around me is in euphoric adulations of our Risen King. And I would have felt like a real jerk. I mean, He died for my sins, and all that but I would rather be at home in jammies, with a new issue of *Coastal Living*. Sooo selfish, I know. But the whole thing is just spiritually weird for me, and I hate going. Have I mentioned that before?

EASTER

Luckily Tim told me to stay in bed and rest because of my cold. Really, I did sound pretty snotty and congested. We are talking Dristan commercial here. Out of guilt, I asked him twelve times if he was sure. As much as I'm not into this whole thing, I don't want Tim to feel like a single parent, and alone at church because I'm not with him. He assured me it was okay, and I fell back into a very deep sleep and didn't wake up again till they came home.

Sitting up in bed and reaching for the tissues I ask, "How was it?" Tim was already unbuttoning his dress shirt and walking into his closet to change his clothes. "Nice. People asked for you. No confetti canon this year but the drums and crosses would have freaked you out. I'm going to go mow the lawn."

20
CONVERSATIONS

"NEVER EVALUATE A RELATIONSHIP BASED ON WHERE IT IS TODAY BUT ON WHERE IT IS GOING."
— ANDY STANLEY.

I finally went to the doctor. It's a sinus infection. I can barely talk. Something about drainage and vocal chords.

My voice sounds like I've been smoking for 30 years. It reminds me of that bit Billy Crystal used to do about his aunt in Florida with the raspy voice: "We live in Boca Raton now. (Long drag on her cigarette) Lenny, get the car… We have the Pompano in the bag. How can a fish in a bag taste so good? Forget

JEW IN THE PEW

about it. (Another long drag) Lenny, get the car... "
I just came downstairs to make myself some chicken soup when the phone rang. It was Rick. He often calls while he's walking to catch the subway to or from work. In the background are typical New York City noises — horns, traffic, people, etc. His conversations are always interrupted by things like, "Hey buddy? Are you serious?" or "Yeah, I'd like a... um... hold on a sec" as he stops to order some food.

Our relationship has come such a long way in the last year and I've been really honest with him about my spiritual longing, and pain. It was downright scary, because he has -zero- tolerance for anything Christian or Messianic. But somehow, amazingly, some good came out of sharing all that. Get this. He just told me that even though he thinks "all that religious stuff is total crap," he respects my decisions and how I have faced the past head on. Pretty great, huh? Wow, that meant a lot to me. Rick even went on to thank me for a few insights I shared last week when we talked. I was so excited about this affirmation from my brother coupled with the decongestant I took this morning that I had to go sit down.

I'm so happy about that phone call. When I started this journey, my relationship with my brother, like many other things, was disjointed. Now it's doing so much better. I never expected that part fixed. I feel so grateful, besides I was also able to salvage my soup.

And yet I also feel a little nauseous. I think it's the phlegm. I'm going back to bed.

Cough, cough.

Bedtime. Everything's blurry. I'm sitting in bed holding tissues to my eyes and trying to write because I feel all stirred up, and journaling helps me let some of the steam off.

As the bottles, tubes and jars in my bathroom attest, I take skin care very seriously. But instead of lovingly dabbing on an assortment of lotions while humming and attended by little birds like Cinderella, I slapped on the wrong thing in the wrong place. I had been lost in thought about this evening, and put cuticle remover on my eyelids. Please do not ever make this mistake. Only burning and tearing will result and nothing will happen to your cuticles.

Listen to this startling conversation I had tonight. It's Wednesday, so I had to wait at church while the kids went to youth group to drive them home. There's a potluck dinner beforehand, and people hang around and talk, or go to different classes. Usually, I can arrange carpool so I don't have to be there because I'm not good at generalized and nondescript milling about.

One, I can't stand to be bored and, two, I find those kind of situations often unnerving without a wingman.

JEW IN THE PEW

When the kids ran off to youth group, I managed to have some pleasant conversation with a few people. When that petered out, I found a table and got out some writing I had been working on. Getting busy helps. Soon though, an acquaintance came over to talk. Honestly, I cannot remember how this came up, but she starts talking about me being Jewish and then says, "Yeah, I haven't read the Old Testament in, like, y e a r s ! Leviticus is just so crazy. I mean all those laws." And then makes a sour face like she just sucked on a lemon or smelled expired meat. I stepped up to the plate and went into teaching mode. I explained that all those laws had a reason. It was God's way of making sure Israel looked and acted differently from the surrounding, pagan societies. How else would they have known sin and understood what separated them from God, if it was not for the law that spelled out right and wrong?

In response, Miss Sweet and Perky says dismissively, "Well, thank God I have grace and can forget all that," and practically skips off. I sat there dumbfounded but here's what went on in my head: "Forget all that? Wow, is that a who-cares-about-anything-that-came-before-me mentality! Ya know, there actually is a link between what God started back then with the whole sacrifices for the forgiveness of sin *thang* and your Christian life now but whatever. Oh, by the way, you forgot your pom-poms."

I had recently been playing with the idea that *maybe*, just maybe, I'm not such an alien at church.

Yeah, right. Writer Bernard Malamud said it best, "If you ever forget you're a Jew, a Gentile will remind you." I know she was being dismissive about the *Torah* and not me per se. For that matter, she meant no specific disrespect. She just didn't get it. Probably because she was never taught otherwise. But still. I think I showed considerable restraint in letting the kids finish their evening instead of hauling their butts out of there after that conversation. And, just for the record, that's not bitterness on my part over Buffy the Church Lady's ignorance. I just kind of feel like Charlie Brown, shaking my head, sighing after Lucy pulls the ball out from under him again and asking myself, "What am I doing here?"

It's Shavuot[96] also known as Pentecost. I just brought an armload of flowers in from the garden. Everything is exploding with blooms.

It's late afternoon. Everybody is busy doing their own thing right now: Tim is having a wonderful time tinkering away in the garage. Em is in her room, though from the sound of it she may be rearranging furniture again. Last month, by herself, she hauled the big blue

---

96 *Shavuot is Hebrew meaning "weeks". It is pronounced shah-voo-OAT.*

armchair all the way up to her room from the first floor guest room. I had to admit it looked better where she put it, though I'm not sure how she managed it. Zan went fishing off the dock with his friends, and I just finished bringing in lots of flower cuttings. I have enough flowers for three or four vases to put around the house and on the table. Tradition says the desert suddenly burst into bloom on *Shavuot*[97] when God gave Moses the *Torah*.

I think the name confuses people. *Shavuot* is calculated exactly seven weeks after Passover. Later, it was also called by its Greek name of Pentecost, which means "fifty days" as it begins on the 50th day after Passover. Very few of my Christian friends are even aware that Pentecost is actually a Jewish holiday. A couple of days ago, I asked a good friend of ours when Pentecost occurs. We were sitting out back with our spouses having a nice summertime dinner, all our kids happily having other plans. It was a trick question, because I know he plans on celebrating it when it comes up in the Christian calendar in a couple of weeks. I wanted to see if my pastor buddy was aware that the very same day God sent us the Holy Spirit, was the very same day He gave us the Torah. Just another example of how the Church sought to distinguish itself from the Jewish believers as originally this was one holiday on the same day. Just saying.

---

[97] *Also known as the Feast of Weeks or as Pentecost.*

CONVERSATIONS

I'm finished arranging the flowers and I'm about to start making dinner. Since we aren't going to *Shavuot* services anywhere tonight, we will be celebrating at home. We'll have cheese blintzes because it's traditional and sweet milk is symbolic of the Torah. Also, we'll discuss the parallels between the giving of the Law in Exodus and the giving of the Spirit in Acts. For example, fire and the sound of thunder in the former, and tongues of fire and the sound of rushing wind in the latter. Either way, it's a time of God meeting us. I read somewhere that Passover is God's courtship with His people, but *Shavuot* is the marriage vows. It's also referred to as the time of the *giving* of the Torah, and not of *receiving*, because any days that our hearts are open are the days we receive the Torah. Isn't that lovely?

Just as I was writing that I heard a birdie sound much closer than outside. A chirpy little Finch had flown in the open back door. It perched on a kitchen stools, not two feet away from me. He was just watching me for a minute or so, cocking his tiny head from side to side. Finally I said, *"Gut yuntif* [98] little birdie." And with that he flew back outside.

---

98 *Yiddish for Happy Holiday. Chag Sameach is how you say it in Hebrew.*

With Tim on a trip to Italy

21
FULL CIRCLE

"IN YOUTH WE LEARN, IN AGE WE UNDERSTAND."
— MARIE VON EBNER-ESCHENBACH

Rainy afternoon. Eating leftover Pad Thai from last night's dinner by the back door, so I can enjoy the pitter-patter. Why did it take me so long to discover cilantro?

It just occurred to me that I never wrote about two interesting meetings I attended. Sorry about that. I

JEW IN THE PEW

didn't mean to leave you out of the loop. Last night, Tim and I stopped for dinner at a fun little Asian restaurant before going to an AIPAC[99] meeting to listen to Herb Keinon, the Diplomatic Correspondent for the Jerusalem Post. He was there to give an overview of the broad spectrum of daily life in Israel, past and present wars, and the current political agendas of the major Mid-East players. Mr. Keinon was engaging and articulated a huge amount of information, leaving us wanting to know more than we already do about Israel.

Another plus was that a friend in the Jewish community whom I'd like to know better had invited us to this talk. When I looked around the room full of fellow Jews I saw a handful I knew. I didn't feel like a stranger.

"No Otis, you can't have my food. Besides, it's too spicy for you."

Just a week ago I had gone to another event and heard from another journalist. Our Hadassah chapter brought the 98-year-old dynamo Ruth Gruber. During WWII she was assigned a secret mission from then Secretary of the Interior Harold Ickes, to bring 1,000 Jewish refugees to the U.S. She also was the *only* journalist permitted access to the ship Exodus 1947, which carried 4,500 Jewish war refugees who were denied entrance to (what was then called) Palestine.

---

99 *American Israel Public Affairs Committee, America's leading pro-Israel lobby.*

FULL CIRCLE

This was a crazy situation that was causing an international uproar. Because I love my Gra so much I happen to have a soft spot for old ladies, especially Jewish little old ladies. But really, Ruth Gruber was extraordinary. Her achievements as woman, as a writer and as a Jew are historic. I bought a few of her books and waited in line for her to sign them afterwards with all the flustery gushing of a star struck teenager. Just another example of my coolness. Oh yeah, baby, so hip, so cool... til the almost centenarian walks in the room. Granted she did walk really slowly.

"For the last time, Otis, trust me, you won't like Thai food."

Here's my point though. I do have one. Hearing from these journalists has underscored what I've realized during this year of evaluating who I am, and what is important to me. Pick a country, almost any country. All over the globe and throughout history, wherever Jews have lived as a 'people group' you can find a time within that country when the Jews were restricted, expelled or murdered. This is why the State of Israel is so vitally important to the Jewish people. It is also why it is so important to maintain being Jewish. I challenge anyone to find any other ancient tribe that has maintained a cohesive identity over the millenniums even through, and in spite of, displacement and persecution. You won't find any. God said Jews were going be around until the end of time and I believe Him. But, now what if I just got absorbed into mainstream Christianity and didn't look or act Jewish anymore? What if I let my kids grow up ignorant of all they are, all the rich Hebrew roots of their Bible? Suppose I never instilled in them a commitment and love for their heritage or Israel? And then what if they grew up and did the same with their kids?

I'm done my leftovers and the rain just stopped. I think some changes are in the air.

At the hairdressers. Tomorrow morning I'm taking the kids to a Messianic conference. I haven't been to one in 25 years.

Angie, my hairdresser, and I have finally come up with a good color for my hair. Never one to be bored, here I sit, typing on my laptop while waiting for the chemicals in the tinfoil all around my head to process. A vision of loveliness, I assure you. This appointment was vital for this weekend. I'll explain.

In the last year, as you know, I joined Hadassah, and attended various synagogues and events. I always left a meeting or function with a huge smile on my face — even if I did have to drive an hour there and back. The Jews of Jacksonville are a truly wonderful community. So far, no one I've met seems to mind much that we are raising the kids with the Christian aspect too, because Tim isn't Jewish. But what if he was? We wouldn't then have an easy explanation for the whole church thing. For as much as I tried to get away from it, as much as I have lived within Christendom, and as much as I enjoy other Jewish sects, I can't deny the part of me that is Messianic. And it's occurred to me that I want the kids to see how I grew up.

I have tried and tried to meld and morph, but it doesn't work. In Church I feel like a cultural foreigner and the worship often leaves me spiritually flaccid. At Synagogue I'm nostalgic and proud of my heritage but the joy seems missing. When I hear Messianic music I feel like all the parts of me connect. So this brings me back to Messianic Judaism – there is a need for it, I am convinced of that. I'll readily admit that there are things about it that ruffle feathers and aren't perfect, but you can have that with any denomination or group.

Did you know that it's different in Israel than it is here, average Israeli Jews just don't care that much if someone is Messianic. From what I hear from friends in Israel, the only ones who really mind if someone is Messianic are the ultra-orthodox, who are pretty much enraged with anyone who isn't them. But then again they won't even support Israel's defense by joining the army. They hysterically cry that Messianics will cause the downfall of Judaism. Oh please. The Arab nations that surround Israel have a land mass 640 times that of Israel and their dream is to annihilate the Jews. Right, the few of us who are crazy enough to believe in Jesus are the big problem.

Hold on. I have to go rinse...

Okay, I'm back. Angie is cutting now. I really need this to look good because tomorrow I'm packing up the kids and going to a Messianic conference where I'll see people who haven't laid eyes on me in 25 years. Last time I went, I was a teenager. We went all the time when I was young and it was so much fun. I originally planned this trip to interview one of the attending rabbis for an article. It was a happy assignment because Neil, the Rabbi, had been a dear friend of my grandparents and mom, but I hadn't seen him in forever. Now, though, I am going because it's time to re-engage on a deeper level. I called my friend Sharon last night to ask some last minute questions as she is going, too.

Years ago, when I was young and she was even younger, we were both in the same Messianic congregation in Philly. She is a Messianic recording artist now and it turns out she lives a little less than an hour away from us. We reconnected recently and we are close with her husband and in-laws as well. Hopefully, at the conference I can hang out with her and her family so I won't be alone. Tim is in Mexico for his nephew's wedding and can't get there till Saturday night. I'm going to need a wingman.

Emme and Zan are interested in going and seeing things and people I've told them about, but they tell me they feel apprehensive. I know how they feel. At least I don't have to worry about my how my hair looks.

Good job, Ange, good job.

Still here at the conference. I'm so glad we came. I've found a shady tree to sit under and write. Many years ago, its branches were sparse and now they're thick and full of leaves.

I'm not gonna lie. I was pretty scared about this trip. Last time I saw these people I was a young teenager and things were messy. When you think about it, it's downright gutsy for me to have come. All I can say about those dark years' decades ago is that people wished they had handled things better and when they heard how it affected me, they deeply regretted the pain that was caused. I appreciated that a great deal. It was easy to put it all behind me when I realized that I am older now than many of those people were then. How many of us in our arrogant 20's or 30's thought we knew what we were doing only to cause major problems that could have been avoided, right? I did. So, I forgave and decided to come back and hug people who were once like family. Everyone has been incredibly glad to see me. It's been like a homecoming. Though they haven't killed the fatted calf yet but there's still tomorrow.

JEW IN THE PEW

I can't wait till Tim gets here so I can introduce him around. Meeting people I haven't seen in a quarter of a century is great fun. I saw so many people who knew me way back when I was girl. Ellen texted me during the service last night and asked how it felt. I wrote back "So familiar and nice to be here! The kids have made friends and seem to be having fun, too. :)". I feel so at home in an I-can-finally-relax kind of way. The worship made me happy and I wanted to sing and found myself smiling. I didn't join in with the dancing though, because from my vantage point it looked crowded like a Messianic mosh pit. It didn't matter since I enjoyed praising God from where I was seated. Messianic worship is more Psalm-like in that it focuses on God: His power, His love, and what He has done. There are times in church when I'm distracted that the songs are so egocentric: how *I* feel, *my* this, *my* that. It seemed to impress Zander too since he leaned over to me and shouted, "Mom, I like this music better. It sounds Jewish and it's about God and it's happy."

I have a few minutes before I need to go meet the kids for lunch. Afterwards, Tim should get here. I'd like to bring him back to sit under this tree and tell him all sorts of conversations I've had in the last couple of days. I have to say I am just blown away by how good God is, that this reconnection with Messianic Judaism all worked out. I honestly didn't expect it to go this well nor did I think this tree would have gotten this big.

FULL CIRCLE

July 5th. A birthday bash weekend.

Wouldn't it be great if personal breakthroughs could happen like fireworks? You light a fuse and poof! "Oh that's pretty. Yes, what a good idea. I'll go with that." Then the wind clears away the smoke and you go on with your life and the new way to look at things. If only.

This weekend Rick flew down so we could all celebrate his 45th birthday, Gra's 90th and my niece Gili's 20th together. All three of them fall within 10 days of each other. Yesterday, the 4th of July, the whole family came to our house for the official lunchtime birthday bash — presents, pin the tail on the donkey (you really need to assist the 90 year old with that one.), party hats and a big gooey chocolate fountain. Wish you were there, right? *Par-taay*. By nightfall, everyone had gone back to Jacksonville to see fireworks over their own patch of sky and not get stuck in traffic on the way home. Soon our cul-de-sac was filled with kids, and explosives that are probably outlawed in a few states. Being somewhat against loud concussive noises and the owner of chocolate splattered kitchen I was inside, trying to clean up when Zander came in complaining about the bottom of his feet. "Well, Zan, what do you expect when you light firecrackers with a blow torch in bare feet?" Tim came in a few minutes later looking pleased. He must have just blown something up. "Tim, were you aware that Zander has been out there without shoes. Again?"

This morning Mom, Ellen, Rick and I went to the beach by ourselves. Literally, within minutes of sitting by the water, beach chairs unfolded and coffee only half drunk, we were deep in discussion. It was kind of like a joint therapy session but without the co-pay... except, come to think of it, I did spring for the Starbucks. During yesterday's birthday party someone brought up the old days, the fun, the family times and it made the old wound ache. So, today I had posed to Mom the difficult statement: "I just don't understand how you could have let it all go — the family unity, the husband, the eleven horses in the country, the beautiful house, all of it." Mom was very open about how lonely and profoundly unhappy she had been in her marriage until she had become a believer. At that point she wanted to make it work, but my father didn't. Not that all that was much of a revelation. What my brother said after that was more insightful.

He told some stories of his childhood that I never heard before – sad and lonely ones. I had been too young to accurately remember the times before the breakup and all was not well before, and then had gone to hell after. My perception had been on longing for everyone to be together, like the pictures in that old photo album. I suddenly pictured a new scrapbook filled with today's family. It's true, I haven't raised my kids with the kind of, or as much of, the Jewish influence and training that I wish I had; but they do have a strong, extended family. And that family is very Jewish in its outlook, humor and history. Having my brother around reinforces all that. It was as if an important picture was just added. Just having us all together laughing, telling stories, crying, dealing with a kids or teenager, or eating together makes it okay to let go of that ache for the lost idyllic family of my childhood and see that we may have different paths and issues but we are still that one big, loud, opinionated Jewish family who support and love each other.

I have to say that this morning's conversation was pretty eye opening. Almost firework in the sky kind of eye opening. Hmmm, how 'bout that. I think I have an urge to go light something.

3:41 AM. Can't sleep. Bed is perfectly comfy but I'm not in it. The ticking of our hall grandfather clock echoes in the quiet of the house.

Everyone else is fast asleep, but I'm downstairs sitting in the triangle of light cast from the lamp by the sofa. I'm trying to decide if I want to bother making a cup of tea or not. Maybe I'm still full from dinner. Last night we had planned to go Paul Wilbur's[100] monthly Messianic *Shabbat* service in Jacksonville. It's still an hour away, but everyone enjoys it. Yesterday, however, we never actually got there. We got home from a big trip the night before, the kids were stressed from so much being on the go and by the time Tim came home from work, which was a long day of driving, we would have had to hop back in the car to drive another hour there. It was just crazy and too much. I really wanted us all to want to go, but not under such duress. In the end, the kids happily stayed home in front of the TV. Tim and I went out to dinner so we could talk.

We ate at a nearby, charming restaurant by the bay – softly lit, a little rustic, with coquina walls and exposed beams. Music drifted upstairs to our table from the bar below. Afterwards, we wandered into a gallery that was open late and found a new artist we liked. Even though we discussed some heavy topics about our lives, it turned out to be a wonderful evening. On the short ride home we passed twinkling lights strung in the trees and horse-drawn carriages before crossing the bridge to home. Quaint. Delightful. And only ten minutes away from my bed — which I am *not* in right now.

I found myself awake thinking about going to church in just a few hours. For the last six months,

---

100 *International Messianic recording artist, teacher and worship leader. Oh yeah and a dear friend of ours.*

FULL CIRCLE

I've enjoyed Sunday mornings less and less. Actually, I haven't even been for at least a month and honestly, it was spotty attendance the month before. Tim and I decided we'd go to the less traditional Saturday night service at church, which feels a lot less churchy, on the weeks we don't go to the Messianic Shabbat service. Even with that adjustment though it doesn't solve everything. I will keep teaching my kids about their heritage, and I'll continue to cultivate my own involvement in the Jewish community. I know full well there is no utopian Jewish-Messianic-Christian community, and even if it does exist we don't live there. We live here, in St Augustine, by the beach, in a charming, picturesque, 300-year-old town. And although this isn't location specific, in a lot of ways I have come full circle. I don't worry about letting people at church know I am Jewish and I can walk into any synagogue, be it conservative, reform, or Messianic, and enjoy myself. These are all good things. I think that I can go back to sleep now.

A hot August Friday afternoon. I just set the Challah dough outside for its second rising. It should be ready to braid by the time the kids get home from the beach. Last week they were competing over whose braiding was better. That is a far cry from where we were a year ago with this.

JEW IN THE PEW

One of the best things about making your own bread is kneading the dough, specifically thinking, praying or maybe even singing while doing so. There is something so fundamental, so elemental about the process that it's profoundly nurturing. My hands are now familiar with the act that was once so foreign and unattainable; the feel of the dough when it needs more flour, when it has to be kneaded some more, when it has risen enough, etc. How metaphoric for what I have been trying to create in our home. Over the last year I have consciously been kneading our Jewish roots back into our lives: sprinkling flour on the table, over the dough and through my hands, and working it in – and then resting, and working it in some more.

Originally I wasn't sure what I wanted. Sometimes I wished for specific bread that I didn't know how to make. Many times I thought we would just go hungry, and this experiment of kneading would simply fail. Tonight is *Shabbat* and we don't have plans to invite anyone over, so it will be just us for a regular family *Shabbat* dinner. To achieve ordinary status means familiarity and that makes me so happy. After dinner we may discuss Zander's upcoming *Bar Mitzvah* and what shape that will take. Or maybe we'll talk about whom to invite to our now-annual *Sukkot* party next month. Regular, Jewish life-cycle events. Sure, our family, our particular bread, doesn't fit a regular mold, but I think it will feed us just fine.

EPILOGUE

"WHAT YOU LEARN ON ONE JOURNEY BECOMES THE BUILDING BLOCKS FOR THE NEXT." — TINA FLAHERTY

Although this book is written as if it took place in one year it actually spanned a few. At the onset of this project, I didn't know it would be a book and certainly not in the form it's in. My only plan was to journal throughout a calendar year all the thoughts and pain and humor that came up as I tried to work out some deep family and spiritual stuff inside. I filled up seven journals that year. The following years were spent finding a way to work all that into a book that navigated between funny and heavy stuff, showing frustration without coming across too sarcastic and hard, and teaching without lecturing. It took a long time. By now many years have passed and here is your update.

Sadly, my beloved Gra has passed away. She was 92. Mom, Ellen and I were with her at their house for those last couple of days when we knew the end was coming. It was hard and sweet and intimate and I had to say goodbye to one of the most important people in my life. She was happy to go see Yeshua and talked about that on her way out. Before she died, I promised her that I would continue to uphold our traditions and make sure that family did the same. I still miss her.

Mom is one busy lady. She writes books and is a speaker on the Jewish roots of Christianity. She is a gifted teacher. Frankly, I can't keep up with her. Eventually she did come to events in the Jewish community and she and Isabel have become close friends.

A couple years ago Dad suffered an aortic dissection. It's is a miracle that he is alive today. Very few people with that condition make it to the hospital, no less survive the surgery. Another rare percentage makes it past the recovery period. It's been an amazing gift to have him not just alive and well but, quite frankly, more affirming and sympathetic than he ever was before. The "event," as he calls his brush with death, brought a great deal of healing and closeness between Dad and us three kids — Rick, Ellen and myself.

Ellen got remarried to a wonderful man with two kids of his own and spent the last number of years with a bustling house full of six teenagers! She and I talk every day.

As much as I loved St Augustine, we finally moved closer to Jacksonville. I was made president of my Hadassah chapter and when they found out I was Messianic it went all the way to national headquarters in 72 hours. The verdict came back that I had every

EPILOGUE

right to be there as anyone else. The rule is against proselytizing, which I don't do anyway. My president who oversaw my group (she was in charge of 900+ members in Jacksonville) told me had they asked me to step down she would have resigned because that was not the type of organization she was going to work for. In any event, I stayed and led that group of about 200 for 3 years and met women that I really love. It was a huge honor to serve them and Israel and Hadassah.

Tim is still patient, strong, handsome, kind, smart, creative and all around wonderful. Even after all these years, I can't believe that I get to spend the rest of my life with him and that he wants to do the same with me. There has never been another person who's shown me more of what unconditional love looks like. Tim often says that his life would have been boring without me and he appreciates and enjoys being part of the tribe.

Emme is now in college studying to be a neonatal nurse practitioner. There were some tough teenage years where she wasn't happy with either of her parent's religious heritages. As every kid has a right to do, she's needed to work things out for herself. Em's become an amazingly responsible person. We couldn't be more proud of her. She desperately wanted to go on a Birthright trip to Israel and this past summer she was able to do so. She did tell them that she believes Jesus is the Messiah but wanted to go on the tour to learn more about her Jewishness since she felt she really didn't get the chance she wanted growing up. It was an amazing experience for her and she was really able to see how much she is a part of this Jewish continuum.

Zander is a strapping 16 year old now, full of muscles, independence and ability. He is currently spending most of his summer in Israel on a mission trip and last I heard he doesn't want to come home. During the year he is in JROTC in high school and military seems to be his future. The kid who was covered in mud and dirt for what seemed like years will now spend an hour making sure everything is shined and perfect for inspection. He works two jobs, and is known for always being busy helping, doing, and building.

Otis is still with us (thank God) and continues to gives his little sighs or opinions about our lives. Two years ago we got him a little friend. Nora is a half Dachshund and half Beagle rescue doggie with a sweet and playful personality. She looks like a very little Beagle so together they make a nice matched set. It's especially cute when they snuggle up together or share a toy.

Maybe that should be my next book, a children's story: Otis and Nora.

EXTRAS

"WHATEVER OTHER QUALITIES JEWS MAY POSSESS, LIKABLE OR THE REVERSE, NO ONE WHO KNOWS THEM WELL CAN DENY THAT THEY ARE PERSONALLY INTERESTING. BY THAT I MEAN, ESPECIALLY ALIVE, ALERT, QUICK AT COMPREHENDING PEOPLE OR EVENTS AND AT MAKING PUNGENT OR WITTY COMMENTS ON THEM. ... ONE MIGHT AT TIMES FIND THE RATHER HOTHOUSE FAMILY ATMOSPHERE, WITH IT INTENSITIES AND FRICTIONS, SOMEWHAT TRYING, BUT ONE COULD BE SURE OF NEVER BEING BORED." — ERNEST JONES, BRITISH PSYCHOANALYST (1879-1958)

RECOMMEND BOOKS FOR FURTHER READING

- Robin Sampson and Linda Pierce, *A Family Guide to the Biblical Holidays* (Heart of Wisdom Publishing 1999).

- Athol Dickson, *The Gospel According to Moses: What My Jewish Friends Taught Me about Jesus* (Brazos Press 2003)

- James Carroll, *Constantine's Sword, the Church and the Jews* (Houghton Mifflin 2001).

- Robert Schoen, *What I Wish My Christian Friends Knew about Judaism* (Loyola Press 2004).

- Judith M. Kunst, *The Burning Word, a Christian Encounter with Jewish Midrash* (Paraclete Press 2006)

- Ruth Gruber, *Exodus 1947, the Ship that Launched a Nation* (Sterling Publishing 2007)

- Jonathan Bernis, *A Rabbi Looks at Jesus of Nazareth* (Baker Publishing Group 2011)

THE MONTHS OF THE JEWISH CALENDAR

(courtesy of AskMoses.com)

Although the Jewish New Year falls on the first of the Jewish month Tishrei (around September), the Torah refers to the Jewish months as beginning from Nissan (around March), the month in which the Jewish people left Egypt. So here they are beginning from Nissan:

EXTRAS

1. *Nissan* (March/April) contains the holiday **Passover**.
2. *Iyar*—pronounced ee-yahr—(April/May)
3. *Sivan* (May/June) contains the holiday **Shavuot**.
4. *Tammuz* (June/July)
5. *Av* (July/August) contains the fast day **Tishah B'av**.
6. *Elul* (August/September) month of introspection leading up to the New Year.
7. *Tishrei* (September/October) contains **Rosh Hashanah, Yom Kippur and Sukkot**.
8. *Cheshvan* (October/November)
9. *Kislev* (November/December) contains **Chanukah**.
10. *Tevet* (December/January)
11. *Shevat* (January/February)
12. *Adar* (Febuary/March) contains the holiday of **Purim**.

CHALLAH RECIPE

1 package dry yeast (about 2 1/4 teaspoons)

1-cup warm water (100° to 110°)

3 tablespoons honey

Dash of saffron threads, crushed

3 tablespoons butter, melted and cooled

1-teaspoon salt

1 large egg

3 cups bread flour, divided into 2 ¾ and ¼ cups

Cooking spray, Baking parchment

1-teaspoon water & 1 egg yolk, lightly beaten

- Dissolve yeast in 1-cup warm water in a large bowl; stir in honey and saffron threads. Let stand for 5 minutes. Add melted butter, 1-teaspoon salt, and egg; stir well with a whisk.

- Add 2 3/4 cups flour to yeast mixture, and stir until a soft dough forms. Cover and let stand for 15 minutes.

- Turn dough out onto a lightly floured surface. Knead until smooth and elastic (about 8 minutes); add enough of remaining flour, 1 tablespoon at

EXTRAS

a time, to prevent dough from sticking to hands (dough will be very soft).

- Place dough in a large bowl coated with oil, turning to coat top. Cover and let rise in a warm place (85°), free from drafts, 40 minutes or until doubled in size. (Gently press two fingers into dough. If indentation remains, the dough has risen enough.)

- Punch dough down. Shape dough into a ball; return to bowl. Cover and let rise an additional 40 minutes or until doubled in size.

- Punch dough down; cover and let rest 15 minutes.

- Divide dough into 3 equal portions. Roll each portion into ropes and then braid. Pinch loose ends to seal. Place on a large baking sheet lined with parchment.

- Cover and let rise 20 minutes or until almost doubled in size. Preheat oven to 375°.

- Combine 1-teaspoon water and large egg yolk, stirring with a fork until blended. Uncover loaf, and gently brush with egg yolk mixture.

- Bake at 375° for 30 minutes or until loaf sounds hollow when tapped. Cool on a wire rack.

ABOUT THE AUTHOR

Jenny grew up an ordinary, 20th century, American-Jewish family and has been married to the cute guy who had his locker next to her in 9th grade for twenty-two years. Somehow between her nonconventional-shoot from the hip-emotions on the sleeves upbringing and his white bread-straight-laced-retired Army-fundamentalist Baptist rearing, they've managed to raise two fully functioning and fabulous kids.

The family lives in Ponte Vedra, Florida with two Beagles who spend most of the day on the sofa while Jenny writes on the floor. When not wrestling with words, gardening or walking on the beach, Jenny has worked with various ministries and non-profits in communication and organizational roles.

For more information please go to
www.jennychandler.com

Made in the USA
San Bernardino, CA
16 October 2013